The Vodou Ethic and the Spirit of Communism

The Practical Consciousness of the African People of Haiti

Paul C. Mocombe

University Press of America,® Inc.
Lanham • Boulder • New York • Toronto • Plymouth, UK

Copyright © 2016 by University Press of America,® Inc.
4501 Forbes Boulevard, Suite 200, Lanham, Maryland 20706
UPA Acquisitions Department (301) 459-3366

Unit A, Whitacre Mews, 26-34 Stannary Street,
London SE11 4AB, United Kingdom

Library of Congress Control Number: 2015954817
ISBN: 978-0-7618-6702-9 (pbk : alk. paper)—ISBN: 978-0-7618-6703-6 (electronic)

♾️™ The paper used in this publication meets the minimum requirements of American
National Standard for Information Sciences Permanence of Paper for Printed Library
Materials, ANSI/NISO Z39.48-1992.

Contents

Acknowledgments

I would like to acknowledge Mt. Carmel/Erzulie my personal lwa for her continued love and strength. I extend my gratitude to my grandparents, Saul and Eugenia Mocombe, who taught me the ways of my ancestors and shaped my practical consciousness. Finally, to my wife, Tiara S. Mocombe, who keeps me living.

Paul Camy Mocombe, January 27, 2015

Introduction

In an effort to resolve the structure/agency debate in the social sciences, Paul C. Mocombe (2012, 2013, 2014), building on the structural Marxism of structuration theory, offers his phenomenological structuralism, which posits structure and agency to be a duality and a dualism. Social Structure is the reification of the material relations of production of a society via language, ideology, ideological apparatuses, and communicative discourse (dualism). Within this conception, the origins and nature of human agency or practical consciousness are fourfold—1) the product of the drives of the physical body and brain; 2) impulses of embodied recycled subatomic particles; 3) structural reproduction and differentiation according to the rules of conduct which are sanctioned for the material relations of production; and 4) the deferment of meaning in ego-centered linguistic and symbolic communicative discourse—with those in power positions in the ideological apparatuses of the society as the final arbitrators in determining what actions or practical consciousnesses are allowed to (re) organize and reproduce in the material resource framework where the mode of production, language, ideology, ideological apparatuses, and communicative discourse (what Mocombe calls the *social class language game*) of a social structure is reified. This work applies Mocombe's phenomenological structural sociology to understanding the constitution of Haitian society and practical consciousness as the parallel evolution and reification of two social class language games (form of system and social integration), the Vodou Ethic and the spirit of communism and the Catholic/Protestant Ethic and the spirit of capitalism.

Haiti is not a Francophone country. It is, as the former Prime Minister of Haiti, Laurent Lamothe (2012–2014), opined, "Africa in the Caribbean."[1] The majority, two-thirds, of the social actors who would come to constitute the Haitian nation-state were African-born amongst a minority of mulattoes, *gens de couleur*, creole, and petit-bourgeois blacks (*Affranchis*) on the island interpellated, embourgeoised, and differentiated by the language, communicative discourse, modes of production, ideology, and ideological apparatuses of the West (the Catholic/Protestant Ethic and the spirit of capitalism social class language game). As such, given their interpellation and embourgeoisement via the language (French), communicative discourse, modes of production (slavery, agribusiness, mercantilism, etc.), ideology (liberalism, individualism, personal wealth, capitalism, racialism, private property, Protestant Ethic, etc.), and ideological apparatuses (churches, schools, prisons, plantations, police force, army, etc.) of the West, the latter, Affranchis, became "blacks," dialectically, seeking to recursively (re) organize and reproduce the ideas and ideals, the Catholic/Protestant Ethic and the spirit of capitalism social class language game, of the European whites in a national position of their own amidst slavery, racism, and colonialism. As the colonial administrators informed the ministry of the marine of the Affranchis as early as the 1750s,

> [t]hese men are beginning to fill the colony and it is of the greatest perversion to see them, their numbers continually increasing amongst the whites, with fortunes often greater than those of the whites. . . Their strict frugality prompting them to place their profits in the bank every year, they accumulate huge capital sums and become arrogant because they are rich, and their arrogance increases in proportion to their wealth. They bid on properties that are for sale in every district and cause their prices to reach such astronomical heights that the whites who have not so much wealth are unable to buy, or else ruin themselves if they do persist. In this manner, in many districts the best land is owned by the half-castes. . . These coloreds, [moreover], imitate the style of the whites and try to wipe out all memory of their original state (quoted in Fick, 1990, pg. 19).

Carolyn Fick (1990) goes on to highlight about the report, "[t]he administrator's report went on to predict, somewhat hyperbolically, that, should this pattern continue, the mulattoes would even try to contract marriages within the most distinguished white families and, worse, through these marriages tie these families to the slave gangs from which the mothers were taken" (pg. 19). Fick further notes of the Affranchis,

> [b]y 1789, the *affranchis* owned one-third of the plantation property, one-quarter of the slaves, and one-quarter of the real estate property in Saint Domingue; in addition, they held a fair position in commerce and in the trades, as well as in the military. Circumstances permitting, a few had even "infiltrated" the almost exclusively *grand blanc* domain of the sugar plantation by becoming managers of the paternal estate upon the father's return to Europe or even inheritors of property upon the father's death. . . The *affranchis* imitated white manners, were often educated in France, and, in turn, sent their own children

abroad to be educated. Having become slave-holding plantation owners, they could even employ white contract labor among the *petits blancs* (1990, pgs. 19–20).

As the colonial administrator sarcastically observed the coloreds had an original state, which they were attempting to "wipe out" of their memory. This original state, was not solely a reference to their conditions as descendants of slave laborers or former slaves themselves, but is also a reference to their African practical consciousness. The former, African-born majority, were not blank slates, but brought with them from Africa their African languages, communicative discourses, ideologies, ideological apparatuses, and modes of production (form of social and systems integration), what I am calling the Vodou Ethic and the spirit of communism social class language game, to the island, which they recursively reorganized and reproduced on the plantations and as maroon communities in the provinces and mountains when they escaped (Métraux, 1958; Deren, 1972; Genovese, 1979; Rigaud, 1985; Fick, 1990; Desmangles, 1992; Trouillot, 1995; Bellegarde-Smith and Michel, 2006; Du Bois, 2004, 2012; Ramsey, 2014). As Leslie G. Desmangles (1992) notes of the communities the African majority would constitute,

> These communities were small, formed initially by Africans who congregated along ethnic lines. As the plantations increased in size and required a larger labor force, the number of maroons increased proportionately, so that by the end of the eighteenth century representatives of other ethnic groups joined the communities; soon, they federated to form. . . "maroon republics." By and large, the various ethnic groups represented within each republic formed separate secret societies or fraternities based on ethnic origins. Each secret society possessed its own ancestral traditions, which it poured into the religious and cultural fabric of its republic; in the contact between these different ethnic cultures, the maroons hammered out for themselves new religious beliefs and practices based on the old. . . Hence, marronage can be seen as a phenomenon that bears witness not only to the slaves' political and social resistance to slavery, but also to the preservation and maintenance of widely divergent ethnic religious traditions from different parts of Africa (pg. 35).

The Vodou ceremony of Bois Caiman, August 14th, 1791, was the gathering and unification of representatives of these "maroon republics" to address their grievances against the Catholic/Protestant Ethic and spirit of capitalism of the whites and Affranchis, constitute the Haitian nation based on the Vodou Ethic and the spirit of communism social class language game, and commence the Revolution on August 22nd, 1791 (Genovese, 1979; Fick, 1990). The negotiations of the African maroon leaders with the whites and Affranchis, for more free days for the Africans to work their lots and less institutional violence on the plantations, during the Revolution must be seen as an attempt to balance the two forms of system and social integration as opposed to an internal struggle between the interest of the leaders of the Revolution and that of the masses as proposed by Carolyn Fick (1990). Both sides failing to compromise left the war for independence on the island as a struggle between two forms of system and social integration, the Protestant Ethic and the spirit of capitalism of the whites and Affranchis on the one hand; and the Vodou Ethic and the spirit of communism of the Africans on the other.

Hence, following the Revolution, whereas, the Affranchis would come to recursively reorganize and reproduce their being-in-the-world as structurally differentiated black "other" agents of the Catholic/Protestant Ethic and the spirit of capitalism social class language game seeking equality of opportunity, recognition, and distribution with whites amidst worldwide slavery, racism, and colonialism. The majority of the half million Africans in the mountains and provinces were not blacks, i.e., a structurally differentiated "other" defined within the lexicon of signification of whites based on their skin pigmentation, lack of culture/civilization, and desire to be like whites. They were Africans interpellated and ounganified/manboified by the modes of production, language, ideology, ideological apparatuses, and communicative discourse of their African worldview or structuring structure, i.e., the Vodou Ethic and spirit of communism social class language game, which they reproduced in the provinces and mountains under the leadership of *oungan yo* (priests), *manbo yo* (priestesses), *gangan yo/dokté fey* (herbal healers), and *granmoun yo* (elders) (Métraux, 1958; Deren, 1972; Genovese, 1979; Rigaud, 1985; Fick, 1990; Desmangles, 1992; Bellegarde-Smith and Michel, 2006).[2] Against the Catholic/Protestant Ethic and the spirit of capitalism of the Affranchis with its emphasis on individualism, personal wealth, and capitalist exploitative labor, the Africans sought balance, harmony, and subsistence living. In the words of a racist colonial observer who saw the futility of attempting to establish a regimen of labor that would impose upon the freed slaves of Saint Domingue a European, occidental mode of thought and of social organization, central to which are the virtues of work, in and of itself, of competitiveness, profit incentives, and ever-expanding production; in short, the virtues of the Western capitalist ethic as practiced by the whites and Affranchis,

> Unambitious and uncompetitive, the black values his liberty only to the extent that it affords him the possibility of living according to his own philosophy (quoted in Fick, 1990, pg. 179).

The "philosophy," Vodou Ethic and the spirit of communism, of the blacks diametrically opposed/oppose the Western capitalist ethic of the whites and Affranchis highlighted here by the colonial observer. It is the failure of the Affranchis, once they gained control of the Revolution and subsequently the nation-state and its ideological apparatuses, to either (re)constitute Haiti via the philosophy/practical consciousness of the Africans or eradicate it completely (via their anti-superstitious campaigns) as they sought and seek to reproduce the ideas and ideals (Western capitalist Ethic) of their former colonial slavemasters amidst their own racial-class tensions, between the creole free blacks and the *gens de couleur*, which maintains Haiti, after over two hundred years of independence, as the so-called poorest country in the Western hemisphere.

Following the Haitian Revolution, the majority of the Africans, given their refusal to work on plantations or agribusinesses (*corvée system*), migrated to the provinces and the mountains, abodes of formerly established "maroon republics," and established a "counter-plantation system" (Jean Casimir's term) based on husbandry, subsistence agriculture, and *komes*, i.e., the trade and sell of agricultural goods for income to purchase manufactured products and services. The mulatto elites and petit-bourgeois free blacks, a Francophile neocolonial oligarchy, countered this counter-plantation system through their control of the ports, export trade, and the political apparatuses of the state, which increased their wealth through the taxation of the goods of the African peasants. As Laurent Du Bois (2012) observed of the process, the former enslaved Africans,

[t]ook over the land they had once worked as slaves, creating small farms where they raised livestock and grew crops to feed themselves and sell in local markets. On these small farms, they did all the things that had been denied to them under slavery: they built families, practiced their religion, and worked for themselves. . . Haiti's rural population effectively undid the plantation model. By combining subsistence agriculture with the production of some crops for export, [*komes*,] they created a system that guaranteed them a better life, materially and socially, than that available to most other people of African descent in the Americas throughout the nineteenth and early twentieth centuries. But they did not succeed in establishing that system in the country as a whole. In the face of most Haitians' unwillingness to work the plantations, Haiti's ruling groups retreated but did not surrender. Ceding, to some extent, control of the land, they took charge of the ports and the export trade. And they took control of the state, heavily taxing the goods produced by the small-scale farmers and thereby reinforcing the economic divisions between the haves and the have-nots (pg. 6).

This counter-plantation system the African majority established against the spirit of capitalism social class language game, i.e., economic gain for its own sake, individualism, personal wealth, private property, labor exploitation, etc., of the *Affranchis*, mulatto elites and petit-bourgeois free blacks, who were interpellated, embourgeoised, and differentiated by the mode of production, ideology, and ideological apparatuses of the West, I seek to argue here, was not a reaction to slavery or the material resource framework of the island as presented by Du Bois and Casimir. Instead, it was and is a product of the ideology (*konesans*) of Vodou and its Ethic of communal living or social collectivism, democracy, individuality, cosmopolitanism, spirit of social justice, xenophilia, balance, harmony, and gentleness, which united all of the African tribes shipped to the island during the slave trade. What I am calling the Vodou Ethic and the spirit of communism social class language game of the Africans was, and is, reified and recursively reorganized and reproduced via the ideology of Vodou; its modes of production, *komes*, husbandry, and subsistence agricultural; and ideological apparatuses, lakous or *lakou yo* in Kreyol (*yo* in Kreyol is used to pluralize terms and concepts), *lwa yo*, *ounfo* (temples) peristyles, *sosyete sekré* (secret societies), *vévés*, herbal medicine, proverbs, songs, dances, musical instruments, Vodou magic and rituals, and ancestor worship (See Table 1).

The African Religion of Vodou, in other words, gave rise to the spirit of communism or communal living based on subsistence agriculture, husbandry, and *komes*, which the Africans, acting as both subjects and agents of the language game, transported with them to the Americas (Genovese, 1979; Fick, 1990; Desmangles, 1992). In Haiti, under the leadership of oungan yo (priests), manbo yo (priestesses), gangan yo/dokté féy (herbal healers), and granmoun yo (elders), they recursively reorganized and reproduced this structuring structure and its modes of production via ideological apparatuses, i.e., Lakous, *lwa yo*, peristyles, herbal medicine, proverbs, songs, dances, musical instruments, secret societies, Vodou magic and rituals, vévés, ancestor worship, and ounfo, used to interpellate and ounganify/manboify the human actors on the plantations, in the provinces, and mountains of the island (Métraux, 1958; Deren, 1972; Genovese, 1979; Fick, 1990; Desmangles, 1992; Bellegarde-Smith and Michel, 2006). As such, by communism I do not mean the social relations of production emanating from the dialectical contradictions of capitalist relations of production as outlined by Marx and Marxists of the early twentieth-century. Instead, the *spirit of communism* I refer to here speaks to the agricultural and communal form of individual, social, and material relations (purposive-rationality) produced by the metaphysical, psychological, and sociological logic (*konesans*—knowledge) of the religion of Vodou by which the Africans went about recursively reorganizing and reproducing their material resource framework prior to its interruption by slavery, the slave trade, racism, colonization, and the Affranchis's attempt at nation building based on the language, communicative discourse, ideology, ideological apparatuses, and modes of production of the West. An ethos, the Vodou Ethic and the spirit of communism social class language game, which emphasizes balance, harmony, perfection, and subsistence living over the economic gain for its own sake, individualism, wealth, private property, and exploitative logic of the Catholic/Protestant Ethic and the spirit of capitalism social class language game of the whites and Affranchis (Mé-

Table 1. Differences between the Catholic/Protestant Ethic and the Spirit of Capitalism and the Vodou Ethic and the Spirit of Communism in Haiti

Differences	The Catholic/Protestant Ethic and the Spirit of Capitalism	The Vodou Ethic and the Spirit of Communism
Language	French	Kreyol
Mode (s) of Production	Agribusiness, Manufacturing (Industrial production), and Post-Industrial Service	Subsistence Agriculture, Husbandry, and Komes (Wholesale and retail Trade)
Ideology	Individualism, Capitalism, subject/object thinking, Authoritarianism, racialism, liberalism, private property	Individuality, Social Collectivism, syncretic thinking, Democratic, spirit of social justice, holism
Ideological Apparatuses	Church, schools, police force, army, law, patriarchal family, Prisons, the streets, bureaucratic organization of work	Ounfo, peristyles, dance, drumming, lwa yo, vévés, Secret societies (Bizango, which serve as police forces of The society), ancestral worship, alters Vodou magic
Communicative Discourse	Economic gain for its own sake, wealth, status, upward mobility, class	Balance, harmony, subsistence living, and perfection
Power Elites	Upper-class of owners and high-level executives of businesses And corporations, educated professionals, bureaucrats, Managers, etc.	Oungan/manbo, bokor, gangan, dokté fey, granmoun

traux, 1958; Deren, 1972; Genovese, 1979; Diop, 1981; Rigaud, 1985; Fick, 1990; Desmangles, 1992; Bellegarde-Smith and Michel, 2006). [3]

Using Mocombe's phenomenological structural sociology, this work explores and highlights how the African religion of Vodou and its ethic, i.e., syncretism, spirit of justice, gentleness, materialism, holism, communalism, democracy, individuality, xenophilia, harmony, and balance, gave rise, under the leadership of *oungan yo, manbo yo, gangan yo/dokté fey*, and *granmoun yo*, to the Haitian spirit of communism and the counter-plantation system (Jean Casimir's term) in the provinces, mountains, and urban slums of Haiti, which would be juxtaposed against the Catholic/Protestant Ethic and the spirit of capitalism of the white, mulatto, and petit-bourgeois free black classes of the island. This latter worldview or social class language game, the Catholic/Protestant Ethic and the spirit of capitalism, I go on to argue, exercised by the free bourgeois blacks and mulatto elites, *Affranchis*, on the island undermined the revolutionary and independence movement of Haiti commenced by subjects/agents, *oungan yo, manbo yo* (Vodou priests and priestesses), *gangan yo/dokté fey*, and *granmoun yo* (elders), of the Vodou ethic and the spirit of communism social class language game, and made it the poorest, most racist, and tyrannical country in the Western Hemisphere (See Table 1).

BACKGROUND OF THE PROBLEM

The stance of early human beings vis-à-vis their experiences of the material resource framework, i.e., the earth, gave rise, for the most part, to two dispositions regarding how they reified their existence, i.e., constituted their society (system and social integration), and went about recursively (re) organizing and reproducing their material being-in-the-world (Greene, 2013). In a fruitful and bountiful environment, as early humankind encountered in Africa prior to their migration elsewhere and interbreeding with Neanderthals, a harmonious disposition towards the world took hold, which was juxtaposed against an antagonistic disposition arising from a lack of resources, etc., as was found among Europeans who migrated out of Africa to Europe. According to the pan-African theorist, Cheik Anta Diop (1981, 1988, 1989), as a result of these experiences African and most people of color on the earth shared certain linguistic and cultural commonalities that formed a tapestry that laid the basis for African cultural unity, which was diametrically opposed to the European cultural unity that would develop among the Neanderthals in the barren and harsh environment of Europe.

What Diop calls the Southern Cradle-Egyptian Model emerged among Africans and other people of color who inhabited a hospitable environment: 1) Abundance of vital resources, 2) Sedentary-agricultural, 3) Gentle, idealistic, peaceful nature with a spirit of justice, 4) Matriarchal family, 5) Emancipation of women in domestic life, 6) territorial state, 7) Xenophilia, 8) Cosmopolitanism, 9) Social Collectivism, 10) Material solidarity—alleviating moral or material misery, 11) Idea of peace, justice, goodness, and optimism, and 12) Literature emphasizes novel tales, fables, and comedy. This Southern Cradle-Egyptian Model was diametrically opposed to a Northern Cradle-Greek (European) Model: 1) Bareness of resources, 2) Nomadic-hunting (piracy), 3) Ferocious, warlike nature with spirit of survival, 4) Patriarchal family, 5) Debasement/enslavement of women, 6) City state (fort), 7) Xenophobia, 8) Parochialism, 9) Individualism, 10) Moral solitude, 11) Disgust for existence, pessimism, 12) Literature favors tragedy.

In this work I propose three interrelating theses. First, I argue that the latter, European/Greek model, over time, and with its encounter with Christianity, became reified and recursively reorganized and reproduced as the Protestant Ethic and the spirit of capitalism social class language game as outlined by Max Weber (1958 [2003]), and the former, African model, as the Vodou Ethic and the spirit of communism social class language game outlined above in Diop's work. Second, both models converged on the island of Hispaniola, at the height of the slave trade and African enslavement during the eighteenth century, where the Vodou leadership, *oungan yo*, *manbo yo* (Vodou priests and priestesses), *gangan yo/dokté fey* (herbal healers), and *granmoun yo,* (elders) of the enslaved Africans of Haiti juxtaposed the latter against the former as embodied by whites and the *Affranchis*, mulatto elites and petit-bourgeois free blacks, in an attempt to overthrow it on the island when they commenced the Haitian Revolution in 1791. Finally, it is this dialectical struggle between the modes of production, ideology, ideological apparatuses, and communicative discourse of the Vodou Ethic and the spirit of communism social class language game of the majority of Africans juxtaposed against those of the Catholic/Protestant Ethic and the spirit of capitalism social class language game of the mulatto elites and petit-bourgeois blacks of the island, *Affranchis*, I go on to argue, that maintains Haiti as the so-called poorest country in the Western Hemisphere.

THEORY AND METHOD

Traditional interpretations of the Haitian Revolution, and subsequent to that the constitution of Haitian identity, attempt to understand them, like the constitution of black diasporic and American practical consciousnesses, within the dialectical logic of Hegel's master/slave dialectic (Genovese, 1979; James, 1986; Fick, 1990; Trouillot, 1995; Nicholls, 1979; Du Bois, 2004, 2012; Buck-Morss, 2009; Ramsey, 2014). Concluding that the Haitian Revolution represents a struggle by the enslaved Africans of the island who internalized the liberal norms, values, and rules of their former French masters, for equality of opportunity, recognition, and distribution within and using the metaphysical discourse of their former white slavemasters to convict them of not identifying with their norms, rules, and values as recursively (re) organized and reproduced by blacks. Haitian identity/practical consciousness, as such, was and is a simulacrum, of European practical consciousness and identity, which is universalized and presented as the nature of reality as such. This position, predominantly held by white Westerners, is usually juxtaposed against the postmodern, post-structural, and postcolonial approaches of Haitian and other black bourgeois intellectual elites (i.e., Aimé Césaire), which highlight the hybridity, ambivalence, négritude, syncretism, and *créolité*, of the Revolution and Haitian consciousness (Genovese, 1979; Fick, 1990; Desmangles, 1992; Trouillot, 1995; Bellegarde-Smith and Michel, 2006).

Both interpretations, contrary to the position of Haitian intellectuals such as Jacques Roumain (1940) and Jean-Price Mars (1928), who advised the Haitian intelligentsia class to look to the provinces and the peasant classes to constitute Haitian culture, identity, and nation-state, are problematic in that they are ethnocentric and racist. They both overlook the initial African practical consciousness of the majority of the Africans on the island for either the practical consciousness or discourse and discursive practices of the mulatto and petit-bourgeois black elites, *Affranchis*, looking (because of their interpellation and embourgeoisement) to Europe, Canada, and America for equality of opportunity, recognition, and distribution, or for their (Affranchis) logic of postmodern, post-structural, and postcolonial theories to undermine that African presence in favor of notions of hybridity, créolité, négritude, syncretism, intersectionality, double consciousness, etc.

In their assumption of control of the state and its ideological apparatuses, i.e., schools, churches, police force, laws, military, etc., in other words, the Affranchis, as the whites before them, attempted to repress, "silence," through anti-superstitious laws to outlaw Vodou and economic policies to undermine its mode of production, the Vodou Ethic and the spirit of communism social class language game of the Africans for their own Euro-centered purposive-rationality, even though, paradoxically, many of them exercised aspects of the latter in secrecy (Fick, 1990; Desmangles, 1992; Trouillot, 1995; Du Bois, 2012; Ramsey, 2014). Furthermore, their dialectical, postmodern, post-structural, and post-colonial textual productions, as seen in the works of Louis-Joseph Janvier, Thomas Madiou, Beaubrun Ardouin, Hérard Dumesle, and Anténor Firmin among many others, minimized and minimize the African structuring structure to highlight hybridity, créolité, négritude, ambivalence, and contradictions. In other words, they accentuate and substantiate the European practical consciousness as recursively reorganized and reproduced by whites, mulattoes, and petit-bourgeois blacks, but minimize the African in the ambivalence, creole, négritude, and hybrid language of postmodern, post-structural, and postcolonial discourses, which are still, dialectically, Western in origins and constitution.

There is no creole, négritude, ambivalent, hybrid, etc., consciousness by which Haitians reified and reify their social structure and went/go about recursively reorganizing and reproducing its ideas and ideals as their practical consciousness. Instead, Haitians, the minority Affranchis, either recursively reorganize and reproduce as an "other" the ideas and ideals of the Republican state, the Catholic/Protestant Ethic and the spirit of capitalism social class language game, as their practical consciousness or those of the Vodou Ethic and the spirit of communism of the mass majority.[4] Postmodern, post-structural, and postcolonial discourses are the language, ideology, and communicative discourse of post-industrial Catholic/Protestant capitalist social relations of production recursively reorganized and reproduced by the Affranchis in the language of créolité, hybridity, indigénisme, négritude, double consciousness, etc., for equality of opportunity, recognition, and distribution with their former colonizers and slavemasters. That is to say, ambivalence, hybridity, liminality, créolité, négritude, double consciousness, etc., are the psychological processes, concepts, pathologies, and practical consciousness of the Affranchis bourgeoisies as they desire and struggle for equality of opportunity, recognition, and distribution with whites by reproducing their ideas and ideals as their practical consciousness in order to convict them (whites), amidst their racism and discrimination, for not identifying with their values and norms as revealed by black practices. As though by highlighting their alleged ambivalence, double consciousness, négritude, and syncretism as opposed to the singular "African" otherness, reflected in the practical consciousness of the masses, which allowed for them to be discriminated against to start with, affords them, Affranchis, their desires (equality of opportunity, recognition, and distribution) and the sympathy of whites.

Using Mocombe's phenomenological structural sociology, to account for the constitution of consciousness and identity (practical consciousness) as a duality and dualism based on the structural reproduction and differentiation of the mode of production constituted via language, ideology, ideological apparatuses, and communicative discourse that discriminate against alternative practical consciousnesses, communicative discourses, ideologies, and ideological apparatuses. In this work, I undertake an "ideal type" analysis of the sociohistorical origins and nature of the originating moments of the Haitian Revolution and contemporary Haitian consciousness within the French and subsequent American dominated global Protestant capitalist bourgeois social structure/world-system. Specifically, I reinterpret the historiography of how the institution of slavery, the slave trade, racism, and colonization impacted, shaped, and re-shaped African practical consciousnesses in Haiti. Beginning in the sixteenth century, Africans were introduced, interpellated, embourgeoised, and differentiated into an emerging global Protestant (liberal) bourgeois capitalist social structure as slaves, mulattoes (*gens de couleur*), creoles, blacks, and petit-bourgeois blacks. Given their economic material conditions, their African practical consciousnesses, what I am calling the Vodou Ethic and the spirit of communism social class language game and its ideology, ideological apparatuses, modes of production, and communicative discourse as constituted by *oungan yo, manbo yo, gangan yo/dokté fey,* and *granmoun yo,* were represented by European whites as superstitious, primitive, animistic, and informal forms of being-in-the-world to that of the emerging dominant white Protestant (capitalist) bourgeois social order with the ever-declining significance of Catholicism following the Protestant Reformation (Weber, 1958[2003]; Patterson, 1982; James, 1986; Fick, 1990; Du Bois, 2004, 2012).

From this sociohistorical perspective, I illustrate the structural forces—religion, race, class, and status—that eventually, under the "contradictory principles of marginality and integration" (Patterson, 1982, pg. 46), (re) shaped a *minority* of African consciousness in Haiti as a "racial class-in-itself" (blacks), a "racial caste in class," divided between a minority group of mulatto elites and free bourgeois blacks (who I am calling the *Affranchis*) who, given their differentiation, interpellation, and embourgeoisement via the church, French schools, language, social roles, class, race, ideology, and ideological apparatuses looked to white (*blancs*) Catholic liberal France for equality of opportunity, recognition, and distribution, on the one hand. And on the other, a *majority* of Africans and first generation Haitians (creoles and maroons) in the provinces, mountains, and enslaved on large plantations, interpellated and ounganified/manboified under the leadership of *oungan yo, manbo yo, gangan yo,* and *granmoun yo,* looking to hold onto, and recursively reorganize and reproduce their African traditions and religiosity (philosophy), the Vodou Ethic and the spirit of communism social class language game, its ideological apparatuses, i.e., peristyles, Lakous, secret societies, etc., and modes of production, *komes*, husbandry, and subsistence agriculture.

This embodiment or forced internalization, embourgeoisement, of liberal bourgeois Catholic/Protestant racial ideas and ideals among the mulatto elites and black petit-bourgeois minority in Haiti, I conclude, in keeping with traditional readings of the Haitian Revolution, eventually made the struggle to obtain equality of opportunity, distribution, and recognition with their white liberal Catholic bourgeois French counterparts amidst racial and class discrimination their goal. This goal, brilliantly embodied in the personhoods of Vincent Ogé, Pierre Pinchinat, Toussaint Louverture, Alexander Pétion, André Rigaud, Jean-Pierre Boyer, Henri Christophe, and the majority of the political and economic elites of Saint Domingue/Haiti turned a minority group of mulatto elites and free blacks on the island into Haitians, in the words of Frantz Fanon (1963), with "black skins and white masks." A Francophile neocolonial oligarchy, who like their white counterparts, discriminated against the mode of production, language, communicative discourse, ideology, ideological apparatuses, religiosity (Kreyol, African, and Vodou), and practical consciousnesses of the newly arrived and enslaved Africans (pejoratively referred to as Congos and Bossales) on the island who were seeking, under the leadership of *oungan yo, manbo yo, gangan yo,* and *granmoun yo,* to recursively reorganize and reproduce their African worldview via their subsistence agricultural mode of production, husbandry, and *komes*; Vodou Ethic and ideology; and ideological apparatuses, i.e., Lakous, *lwa yo*, peristyles, herbal medicine, proverbs, songs, dances, musical instruments, ounfo, ancestor worship, etc.

As such, contrary to the logic of postmodern, post-structural, and post-colonial theories, whose concepts constitute the practical consciousness and psychology of the Affranchis, my position is that the majority of the Africans of Haiti did not (re) produce a creole, syncretic, and hybrid culture in the mountains, provinces, and urban slums. They recursively reorganized and reproduced an African mind or structuring structure (form of system and social integration), which incorporated under the leadership of their power elites other concepts and processes in their form of system and social integration, the Vodou Ethic and the spirit of communism social class language game, as it stood against the Catholic/Protestant Ethic and spirit of capitalism social class language game of the whites and Affranchis. Créolité, hybridity, etc., emanates from the practical consciousness of the Affranchis using the theoretical logic of postmodern, post-structural, and postcolonial theories to Westernize the African structuring structure (which is recognizable and acceptable by whites) for equality of opportunity, recognition, and distribution with their white counterparts. Hence their (the *Affranchis*) subsequent usurpation, with the assassination of Jean-Jacques Dessalines in 1806, of the Haitian Revolution and nation-state from the newly arrived and enslaved creole/Kreyol Africans on the island who commenced it on August 14th, 1791 at Bois Caiman, turned the aim of the Revolution and Haitian consciousness towards the substantive and purposive-rationality, i.e., economic gain, status, and power, of the Affranchis. They (mulatto elites and petit-bourgeois blacks) dialectically attempted to achieve equality of opportunity, recognition, and distribution with whites, by convicting and attempting to repress the society for not identifying with their norms and values (the norms and values of the French initially and subsequent to them the Americans), which the *Affranchis* embodied and recursively (re) organized and reproduced in their practices as an "other." Against the Vodou ethic and the spirit of communism (what Jean Casimir calls the counter-plantation system) social class language game of the Vodou leadership of the masses of Africans in the provinces and mountains of the island, the Affranchis sought to establish a capitalist periphery state within the capitalist world-system based on agribusinesses and exportation initially, and subsequent to that tourism and textile manufacturing performed by the Africans. The latter, Africans, in the Western logic of the Affranchis became superstitious masses and peasants whose practical consciousness was co-opted and commodified to entertain tourists, and their labor power were/are exploited as wage-laborers in white-owned, and Affranchis administered, factories and agribusinesses.

Conversely, the Haitian Revolution as initiated on August 14th, 1791 at Bois Caïman by *oungan*, Boukman Dutty, and *Manbo*, Cecile Fatiman, Edaïse, etc., was led by the African-born majority, under the leadership of *oungan yo, manbo yo, gangan yo*, and *granmoun yo* (elders) seeking to recursively reorganize and reproduce their African/Taino practical-consciousness in the world against the Catholic/Protestant bourgeois liberalism and capitalism of whites and the *Affranchis* class of Haiti, who would subsequently, with the assassination of *oungan* Jean-Jacques Dessalines in 1806, undermine that attempt for a more liberal and French purposive-rationale, similar to that of the black American civil-rights movement, which would reintroduce wage-slavery and peonage on the island. As Eugene Genovese brilliantly highlights in his work, *From Rebellion to Revolution* (1978), it is this initial, "restorationist," divergent path against slavery and liberal bourgeois Catholicism/Protestantism that sets the majority of Haitian practical-consciousness and the originating moments of the Haitian Revolution under the leadership of *oungan yo, manbo yo, gangan yo*, and *granmoun yo* apart, as a distinct phenomenon, from the bourgeois desires and purposive-rationale of the *Affranchis* in Haiti and liberal black Protestant bourgeois male preachers of America and the diaspora, seeking to serve as the bearers of ideological and linguistic domination for the so-called black masses by recursively reorganizing and reproducing the agential moments of their former white slavemasters and colonizers.[5] To only highlight the latter, liberal bourgeois Protestant/Catholic initiative, or submerge the former, originating moments of the Haitian revolution under the Vodou leadership of *oungan yo, manbo yo, gangan yo*, and *granmoun yo*, under the purview of a Hegelian master/slave universal dialectic—as so many theorists, including the work, *Black Jacobins*, of CLR James (1986), and Susan Buck-Morss's (2009), *Hegel, Haiti, and Universal History*—or the (Affranchis) logic of post-modern, post-structural, and postcolonial theories is to deny the existence of the African practical-consciousness that has been seeking to constitute its practical consciousness in the world since the beginning of the slave trade, worldwide racism, and slavery in favor of the liberal bourgeois Protestantism/Catholicism of whites, petit-bourgeois blacks, and the mulatto elites.

Fortunately, the Affranchis have yet to stamp out, as was done to the blacks in America and elsewhere in the Caribbean, the African linguistic system, Creole/Kreyol, and practical-consciousness, Vodou Ethic and the spirit of communism, of the Haitian/African people. In fact, it is this continuing struggle between the Western ideas and ideals of the mulatto elites and petit-bourgeois blacks fighting for control of the state and its ideological apparatuses on the one hand, against the leadership of the African people in the provinces and mountains seeking to recursively reorganize and reproduce their Vodou Ethic and the spirit of communism on the other that plagues

Haiti today within the American dominated Protestant capitalist world-system.

DISCUSSION AND CONCLUSION

The aim of this work is to relationally examine the origins and purposive-rationale of the Vodou Ethic and the spirit of communism social class language game and the originating moments of the Haitian revolution vis-à-vis the purposive-rationality, the Catholic/Protestant Ethic and the spirit of capitalism social class language game, of the *Affranchis* who would come to dominate the Revolution, the African people, and the state with the help of French, Canadian, German, and American merchants and capitalists. The book will identify their ideological and practical divergent paths, which, contemporarily, has made the former, the African Haitians, the pariah of the West and the latter, the mulatto elites, petit-bourgeois blacks, and foreign merchant class in Haiti, colonizers, i.e., a Francophile neocolonial oligarchy. The argument here is that the purposive-rationality of the originating moments of the Haitian Revolution at Bois Caïman originates out of the Vodou ethic and the spirit of communism social class language game of the masses and their Vodou leadership, *oungan yo, manbo yo, gangan yo/dokté fey,* and *gran moun yo,* and diametrically opposed the purposive-rationality of the liberal agents of the whites and *Affranchis* on the island. The latter three sought to recursively reorganize and reproduce the practical consciousness of their former white slavemasters for equality of opportunity, distribution and recognition, while the agents of the former did not. Instead, at Bois Caïman, the originating moment of the Haitian Revolution, Boukman Dutty, Cecile Faitman, Edaïse, and subsequent to them Macaya, Sans Souci, Sylla, Mavougou, Lamour de la Rance, Macaque, Alaou, Coco, Sanglaou, and Jean-Jacques Dessalines among many others, sought to recursively reorganize and reproduce their African practical consciousness, Vodou, Kreyol, and communism embedded in the counter-plantation system, husbandry, and *komes* of the Haitian/Africans against the purposive-rationality of their former slavemasters and the *Affranchis.* In fact, my argument concludes by suggesting that it is the usurpation of the Revolution by the *Affranchis* that would give the Revolution (and Haitian consciousness/identity) its (postmodern, post-structural, postcolonial) liberal bourgeois Catholic/Protestant orientation, which makes Hegel's master/slave dialectic, postmodern, post-structural, and postcolonial theories appropriate heuristic tools for understanding the subsequent developments of the Haitian Revolution and nation-state following Bois Caïman and the death of Jean-Jacques Dessalines in 1806. This (postmodern, post-structural, postcolonial) liberal bourgeois Catholic/Protestant orientation is the basis for the subsequent exploitation and oppression of the

African masses on the island by the *Affranchis* seeking, like their black American and diasporic counterparts, continual equality of opportunity, recognition, and distribution with their former white masters through the reenslavement (via the tourist and textile industries, sports, and agribusinesses) of the African masses who grow poor and sick so that a few of their fellow citizens can live lavishly within the liberal bourgeois Protestant capitalist world-system under American hegemony.

This latter traditional liberal bourgeois (postmodern, post-structural, and postcolonial) interpretation of the Haitian revolution and the purposive-rationality of the Affranchis attempts to understand their denouement through the sociopolitical effects and dialectical logic of the French Revolution when the National Constituent Assembly (*Assemblée Nationale Constituante*) of France passed *la Déclaration des droits de l'homme et du citoyen* or the Declaration of the Rights of Man and Citizen in August of 1789. The understanding from this perspective is that the enslaved Africans, many of whom could not read or write French, were a blank slate who understood the principles, philosophical and political principles of the Age of Enlightenment, set forth in the declaration and therefore yearned to be like their white masters, i.e., "freemen and women" seeking liberty, equality, and fraternity, the rallying cry of the French Revolution. Although, historically this understanding holds true for the mulattoes and free educated blacks, *Affranchis,* who used the language of the declaration to push forth their efforts to gain liberty, equality, and fraternity with their white counterparts while attempting to hold on to slavery. This position, however, is not an accurate representation for the 201 representatives of the one Taino and nineteen enslaved African tribes/nations, "maroon republics," and their Vodou leadership who organized and assembled (*minokan* in Vodou) at Bois Caïman, Macaya, Sans Souci, and Jean-Jacques Dessalines who would assume the reins of the Revolution following the capture and death of the *Affranchis*, Toussaint Louverture.

Although Dessalines, unlike Sans Souci, Macaya, and many of the African leaders who assembled at Bois Caiman, was an "illiterate" (in the Western sense) creole, the argument highlighted by oral historian Byyaniah Bello and the Vodou community is that as a field slave, he was interpellated and ounganified (my term for internalization of the Vodou worldview) by the ideology (Vodou) and ideological apparatuses (Lakou, peristyles, lwaes, Kreyol proverbs) of the Africans as opposed to the ideology and ideological apparatuses of the French and *Affranchis*. As such, his early (1804–1806) reins as emperor of the country was an attempt, like the Africans of the maroon republics who negotiated with the whites and Affranchis during the Revolution, to constitute a new nation-state amidst two opposing worldviews or structuring structures, the Vodou Ethic and spirit of communism of the African masses and their leadership on the one hand, and the Catholic/Protestant Ethic and spirit of capitalism of the *Affranchis* on the other. Dessalines did not simply attempt to recursively reorganize and reproduce the ideas and practices of the whites as embodied in the ideology and practices of the Catholic/Protestant Ethic and spirit of capitalism as I am suggesting that the *Affranchis* would do in constituting the Haitian nation-state following his death. Instead, he attempted, with the aid of his *lwa mèt tèt* (Vodou spirit), Ogou Feray, to weigh and reconcile the ideals of both worldviews amidst their antagonism as represented by the Affranchis desire for a liberal/capitalist state based on plantation export agriculture, and the subsistence agriculture, husbandry, and *komes* of the African masses.

Conversely, the Affranchis, embodied in the persons of Toussaint, Boyer, Pétion, and Christophe, for examples, like their black bourgeois counterparts in North America and the diaspora, pushed for liberty, equality, and fraternity with their white counterparts at the expense of the Vodou, communal discourse, and Kreyol language of the Vodou leadership, *oungan yo*, *manbo yo*, *gangan yo*, and *granmoun yo*, who were not only discriminated against by whites but by the slave-owning mulattoes and free blacks as well who sought to reproduce the French language, Catholic Religion, and liberal capitalist (mercantile) laws of their former slavemasters on the island. In fact, what role should mulattoes and free blacks play in the Revolution is at the heart of a bitter disagreement between Toussaint and Dessalines. The latter, Dessalines, a *oungan*, Vodou priest, given the brutality he experienced as a field slave, which stood in contradistinction to Toussaint's experience as a literate free *Affranchis*, wanted to kill many of the free and mulatto *Affranchis* along with the whites because Dessalines discerned that they played a role in their yearning to be like their white counterparts in oppressing the enslaved African masses, and given the opportunity they would reproduce the slavery system and the ideas (structuring structure) of the whites on the island (Du Bois, 2004, 2012; Buck-Morss, 2009). Hence Dessalines, like the African Jeannot who Toussaint and Jean Francois would murder for his brutality against the whites, promoted a form of racial slaughter grounded in "an eye for an eye" ethical discourse, "we have rendered to these true cannibals [(the whites)], war for war, crime for crime, outrage for outrage; yes, I have saved my country: I have avenged America" (Jean-Jacques Dessalines cited in Morss, 2009, p. 143).

It is not enough, however, to view Dessalines's discourse and discursive practices along the inverted black-nationalist and pan-Africanist lines of Marcus Garvey, Malcolm-X, Henry Highland Garnet, Martin Robinson Delaney, and W.E.B. Du Bois as highlighted by Susan Buck-Morss (2009) and David Nicholls (1979). To do so, would make his position a structurally differentiated dialectical response to enslavement, i.e., an "other" seeking to recursively reorganize and reproduce the Catholic/Protestant Ethic and the spirit of capitalism in a national/racial position of his own. My position here is that his response, like the Africans Jeannot's and Sans Souci's positions, was "enframed" by the structuring logic, Vodou Ethic and spirit of communism social class language game, of the masses and their Vodou leadership on the one hand and that of the *Affranchis* on the other. As such, his movement as highlighted in the discourses of the Haitian oral historian Byyaniah Bello and *Vodouizan*, Max Beauvoir, was not only racial, but it was also class-based enframed by the cultural and structural logic of the Vodou ethic and the spirit of communism as constituted at Bois Caiman as it stood against the spirit of capitalism of the whites and *Affranchis*. Dessalines, under the guidance of his Vodou *lwa mét tét* (Vodou spiritual guide), Ogou, was seeking land and economic reform, racial and cultural pride, and social justice for the African masses on the island "whose fathers were in Africa" at the expense, some believe, of the interests of the mulatto elites and petit-bourgeois black property owners on the island who assassinated him for doing so (Dupuy, 1989; Nicholls, 1979; Du Bois, 2004, 2012). As Dessalines declared, "the sons of the colonists' have taken advantage of my poor blacks. Be on your guard, negroes and mulattoes, we have all fought against the whites; the properties which we have conquered by the spilling of our blood belong to us all; I intend that they be divided with equity" (Dessalines quoted in Nicholls, 1979, pg. 38).

In order to commence his nationalization project, Dessalines, following the Revolution, did not seek to recursively reorganize and reproduce the Catholic/Protestant Ethic and the spirit of capitalism of the French. Instead, he rejected everything that was French, i.e., language, culture, and system of organizing existence, for the metaphysics and practical consciousness of the Vodou leadership who originated the Revolution. He, guided by Ogou, nationalized the land; disallowed whites, outside of the five thousand polish and Germans who fought with him during the Revolution, ownership of land on the island; amidst state owned plantations he allowed the masses land to reproduce their subsistence agriculture, husbandry, and *komes*; named the island Ayi-ti to honor the Taino natives and African ancestors who spilled their blood during the Revolution; erected a red and black flag to represent the people and the blood they spilled for their freedom; removed all racial and class distinctions by denoting all persons on the island blacks divided between laborers and soldiers; and sought to make the entire island of Ayiti an independent black nation for all blacks in Haiti and the diaspora. As Leslie G. Desmangles highlights,

> [d]uring the first three years after independence (1804–1807) under Jean-Jacques Dessalines's administration, Haiti was united economically and politically. . . At the outset of his administration, Dessalines. . . divided the citizens of the country into two categories, the laborers and the soldiers. Fearing the return of the French army, Dessalines. . . organized all those who had actively

participated in the war of independence into an army of 25,000 men. . . . Those who had been on the plantations during the war continued as laborers and cultivated the large acreages the government had annexed from the white planters. . . . The newly militarized agriculture. . . produced largely sugar, cotton, and coffee, which mulatto overseers divided according to certain state-established criteria. . . The overseers were to transmit one-half of the crops to the state: one half of this was used for export, and the other half paid the rent on the land. Another quarter of the total crop yield was retained for the workers' salaries, and the remaining quarter paid the salary of the plantation overseers (1992, pgs. 38–39).

These efforts, i.e., his eye for an eye morality, establishment of an empire ruled by an oungan, honoring the Taino and African ancestors, social justice, communal living, social collectivism, equitable distribution of resources and salaries, and consultation with his *lwa mét tét*, etc., which the Affranchis deplored as it took away their properties and status, were a by-product of his interpellation and ounganification/manboification via the ideology and ideological apparatuses, Lakou, peristyles, etc., of the Vodou Ethic, and not an arbitrary reaction to his treatment as a field slave.[6] In other words, they emanated from his African mind or structuring structure (form of system and social integration), which the Affranchis rejected while in many instances practicing aspects of its religiosity in secrecy.

Unlike Toussaint, who was interpellated and embourgeoised by his slave-master via the church and his schooling, Dessalines was predominantly interpellated and ounganified/manboified in the language, communicative discourse, ideology, ideological apparatuses, and mode of production of his African parents and Aunt Mantou, who were not reactionary natives to their material conditions. Instead, they were agents of the Vodou Ethic and the spirit of communism social class language game, which they went about recursively reorganizing and reproducing on the island via the Vodou religion; its mode of production, subsistence agriculture, husbandry, and komes; and ideological apparatuses, *lwa yo*, lakous, herbal medicine, proverbs, songs, dances, musical instruments, ounfo, and peristyles. They interpellated and ounganified/manboified Dessalines within the aforementioned practical consciousness amidst his interpellation in the Western structuring structure as a field slave, which he would escape from when he turned 30 years of age. Dessalines, following his escape, continued his ounganification/manboification in the African maroon communities of the North under the leadership of Francois Papillon, Jeannot, and Georges Biassou. As such, with his assumption of the leadership of the Haitian nation-state following the Revolution, Dessalines attempted to constitute it within two opposing structuring structures, the Vodou ethic and the spirit of communism social class language game on the one hand, and the Catholic/Protestant Ethic and the spirit of capitalism on the other, both assuming to represent the nature of reality as

such. That Dessalines would go about suppressing elements of Vodou following the Revolution is not on par with what Toussaint and the rest of the
Affranchis—with the exception of Faustin Soulouque and Francois Duvalier—would go about doing to remove it entirely from the nation-state. Instead, Dessalines attempted to minimize the effects of political instability and
magic done against him by the Petwo elements of Vodou (Desmangles,
1992, pg. 45).[7]

Toussaint, a practicing *gangan/dokté fey* himself, however, also interpellated and embourgeoised by the ideology and ideological apparatuses of the
West, believed that the technical and governing skills of the *blancs* (whites)
and *Affranchis* would be sorely needed to rebuild the country, along the lines
of white civilization, after the revolution and the end of white rule on the
island. In fact, Toussaint was not seeking to constitute the island as an independent country, but sought to have the island remain a French colony without slavery. Hence Toussaint rejected the practical consciousness of the Vodou leadership and the masses for the structuring logic of the West. Although
Dessalines's position would become dominant after the capture of Toussaint
in 1802, his (Dessalines's) assassination by a plot between the mulatto, Alexandre Pétion, and petit-bourgeois black, Henri Christophe, who sought to
pattern their leadership after Toussaint, would see to it that the *Affranchis's*
purposive-rationality would come to historically represent the ideas and
ideals of the Haitian quest for independence and the Republic, which it
produced. After the death of Dessalines,

> the country became divided between north and south, and between two rival
> political factions led by two ambitious men—tyrants who maintained political
> power solely by military force. Henri Christophe crowned himself king of the
> northern kingdom of Haiti in 1807 and ruled until 1820; his political rival
> Alexandre Pétion served as president of the south between 1807 and 1818.
> Haiti was reunited politically in 1822 during the presidency of Jean-Pierre
> Boyer (1818–43), Pétion's former personal secretary and minister. . . In both
> the south and, particularly, the north, the first part of the history of independent
> Haiti is a story of servitude supported by a militarized agriculture whose
> government was drawn from the mulatto class. Their despotic rule early in the
> republic paved the way for the emergence of a rigid new social structure in
> which former affranchis were to become an elite distinctly separated from the
> black masses (Desmangles, 1992, pg. 38).

This purposive-rationality of the *Affranchis*, to adopt the Catholic/Protes-
tant Ethic and spirit of capitalism social class language game of whites by
recursively reorganizing and reproducing their God, language, French, and
exploitative ways of being-in-the-world, liberalism and capitalism, is, however, a Western liberal dialectical understanding of the events and their desire (captured in their postcolonial, post-structural, and postmodern dis-

courses) to be like their white counterparts, which stands against the anti-dialectical purposive rationality of Boukman, Fatima, Edaïse, the rest of the maroon Africans who congregated for the Petwo Vodou ceremony at Bois Caïman/ Bwa Kayiman, and the subsequent positions of Macaya, Sans Souci, and Jean-Jacques Dessalines. (It should be mentioned that many of the African-born soldiers and leaders, such as Jeannot and colonel Jean-Baptiste Sans Souci, distrusted the creole Africans—seemingly because of their desires to be like the whites, vacillations during the war, and ties to the whites—such as Dessalines and Christophe, and in many instances refused to fight under their leadership. In fact, Christophe would murder Sans Souci, and name his famous palace in Milot after him, on the count that he refused to recognize his leadership.).

The events at Bois Caïman and Jean Jacques Dessalines's position, I want to suggest here, do not fit well within the attempt by many Western scholars, blacks and otherwise, to conceptualize the social agency of Dessalines, the African participants of Bois Caïman, and the masses they would interpellate and ounganified/manboified within the Hegelian master/slave dialectical, postmodern, post-structural, and postcolonial thinking of the Affranchis. Instead, the events at Bois Caïman represent an anti-dialectical rejection by the Vodou leadership of white culture, language, God, mode of production, ideology, and ideological apparatuses for the actualization of their African ethos (structuring structure), the Vodou ethic and the spirit of communism, as a "class-for-itself," a group of people with their own Gods, language, mode of production, ideology, ideological apparatuses, and culture, who rejected the inhumanity of the whites, their gods, ideology, ideological apparatuses, exploitative modes of production, and communicative discourse. What the African Vodouizans insist is that,

> No living person has the right to possess another, for possession means the mounting and the controlling of a person's will. . . It means that the possessed person's gwo-bon-anj is temporarily displaced by the influence of a foreign element whose incommensurable power accords that person the capacity to perform feats that are humanly impossible under ordinary circumstances. The possessed lose their memory, intelligence, and responsibility for their actions, and no living person can impose such a will on the living (Desmangles, 1992, pg. 81).

Be that as it may, the Africans, because of their "philosophy," constantly fought against slavery, and sought to be free with allegiances to Bon-dye, lwa yo, and the Vodou Ethic and the spirit of communism as it stood against the Protestant Ethic and the spirit of capitalism social class language game of the whites and Affranchis.

Sociologically speaking, in other words, two worldviews or ethos (form of system and social integration) for organizing the material resource framework emerged in Haiti during and following the Revolution. Both world-views, the Vodou Ethic and the spirit of communism social class language game on the one hand, and the Catholic/Protestant Ethic and the spirit of capitalism social class language game on the other, are distinct from one another, and the former is neither a structurally differentiated practical consciousness, nor does it emerge out of the dialectical unfolding of the Western worldview. It emanates out of the Vodou metaphysics, psychology, and sociology of the Africans who sought to recursively (re) organize and reproduce it in their new environment. This Haitian/African structuring structure (form of system and social integration) remained on the island, as the dominant discourse and discursive practice, until the death of Jean-Jacques Dessalines when the mulatto elites and petit-bourgeois blacks assassinated him and made dominant the Catholic, aristocratic, and feudal (republican) order of France, and subsequently, the Protestant Ethic and spirit of capitalism social class language game of America. The latter would come to dialectically displace the former, as it stood against the Vodou Ethic and spirit of communism of the Haitian masses, which they (the Affranchis) sought to erase/ "wipe out" by co-opting and incorporating it in the European objects of thought as irrational, backwards, damned, and informal. Albeit the Vodou Ethic and spirit of communism was not eradicated or converted into African-isms as found amongst other blacks in Africa and the diaspora. Instead, it remained in the provinces, mountains, and urban slums reified (via its ideology, ideological apparatuses, and mode of production, which were used to interpellate and ounganified/manboified the masses) as the dominant discourse and discursive practice, i.e., practical consciousness, of the majority of Haitians against the practical consciousness of the Affranchis, who attempted and attempt to replicate French/American practical consciousnesses via the apparatuses of the Haitian state and its ideological apparatuses. Contemporarily, they, the Affranchis, attempt its (the Vodou Ethic and the spirit of communism) incorporation into the state through the postmodern, post-structural, and postcolonial logic of créolité, hybridity, etc. in their continual desire for equality of opportunity, recognition, and distribution with whites, not as an enframing ontology by which to interpellate and constitute the human actors of the state. That is, the Vodou Ethic and the spirit of communism of the masses is co-opted and incorporated in the modes of production, language, ideology, ideological apparatuses, and communicative discourse of the bourgeois state as a means for profit in the capitalist world-system under American hegemony where it is used to entertain tourists.

    This work, in the end, explores the black racism and classism by which the Haitian mulatto and free black petit-bourgeoisie, like their white counter-parts, sought and seek to constitute the Haitian nation-state of Haiti by discriminating against and marginalizing the economics, ethic, and linguistic system, creole/kreyol, of the African masses on the island, which remains in the provinces and practical consciousness of every Haitian under the leadership of *oungan yo, manbo yo, gangan yo,* and *granmoun yo.*

The term black is used here to refer to people of African descent in the diaspora, that is, America and the Caribbean. The present author will also use the term black culture generically throughout the course of this work to describe diasporic cultures. Moreover, Kreyol terms will be used interchangeably with their French counterparts. For example, in some instances I will utilize Bwa Kayiman (Kreyol) for Bois Caïman (French), loas (French) Lwa (kreyol), Kreyol, etc. The intent is not to confuse the reader; instead, it is in part to highlight the linguistic dynamics of the Haitian people amidst the discriminatory effects of the mulatto elites and petit-bourgeois blacks. Lastly, the term *Affranchis,* as in the work, *The Making of Haiti: The Saint Domingue Revolution from Below,* of Carolyn Fick (1990), will be utilized to represent both the mulatto elites and free petit-bourgeois blacks. The logic here is that their interpellation and embourgeoisement via the ideology and ideological apparatuses of the West renders their practical consciousness identical amidst their class and racial tensions. I have also chosen to highlight the purposive-rationality or structuring structure of the Affranchis as the Catholic/Protestant Ethic and the spirit of capitalism social class language game to accentuate the fact that although they would adopt the Catholic religion of the French, they exercise their Catholicism as agents of the Protestant Ethic and the spirit of capitalism, the emerging practical consciousness or purposive-rationality of modernity. Modernity, for me, building on the work of Max Weber (1958 [2003]), simply reflects the ever-increasing rationalization of a form of Protestant Christianity via the discursive practices of capitalist relations of production. As such, the purposive-rationality of the Affranchis, like their white counterparts, became, and is, economic gain for its own sake, wealth, etc. Albeit, contemporarily, with the prosperity discourse coming out of post-industrial Protestant capitalist relations of production economic gain for its own sake coupled with material wealth as a sign of God's grace and blessings dominates the ethos.

The underlining hypothesis of the work is that the early freedom and reluctance of the Haitian/African-born masses, under the leadership of *oungan yo, manbo yo, gangan yo/dokté fey,* and *granmoun yo,* to adopt the western metaphysics of their former colonizers over their own structuring structure made them pariahs of the global capitalist world-system discriminated-against by both black and white agents of the emerging Protestant Ethic and the spirit of capitalism world-system. Initially, the work will assess the theoretical basis regarding the constitution of black cultural and religious identity in Haiti and the black diaspora. This theoretical reevaluation will be followed by chapter two which will present an alternative, structurationist, methodological and theoretical framework, phenomenological structuralism, within which to understand the constitution of modernity as the Catholic/

Protestant Ethic and the spirit of capitalism and Haitian cultural and religious life in Haiti as the Vodou Ethic and the spirit of communism. Chapter three provides an historical overview of a structurationist interpretation of the constitution of modernity as the Protestant Ethic and the spirit of capitalism; and chapter four does the same for Haitian/African practical consciousness as the Vodou Ethic and the spirit of communism. Chapter five explores and highlights the convergence of the Catholic/Protestant Ethic and the spirit of capitalism and the Vodou Ethic and the spirit of communism on the island of Hispaniola, and how the former was used to attempt to overthrow, oppress, and discriminate-against the latter. In other words, the origins and constitution of Haitian cultural and religious life as the Vodou Ethic and the spirit of communism, which led to the Haitian Revolution will be assessed and evaluated against the Protestant Ethic and spirit of capitalism of modernity and the Affranchis. The chapter concludes the work by highlighting how the Catholic/Protestant Ethic and the spirit of capitalism social class language game of the mulattoes, petit-bourgeois blacks, and foreign merchant elites, who would come to gain control of the ideological apparatuses of the nation-state of Haiti following the Revolution underdeveloped the island, and made it the so-called poorest country in the Western hemisphere against the Vodou Ethic and the spirit of communism social class language game of the Haitian masses under the leadership of *oungan yo, manbo yo, gangan yo*, and *granmoun yo*.

NOTES

1. Former Prime Minister Laurent Lamothe speaking at the 22nd Ordinary Session of the African Union, which took place in Addis Ababa, Ethiopia January 30, 2014.

2. I use the terms, ounganified/manboified, similar to how Althusser utilizes the term "embourgeoisement" as it pertains to the socialization process in the "Catholic/Protestant Ethic and spirit of capitalism social class language game" (my term) of the West. Albeit in my usage ounganified/manboified refers to socialization within the Vodou Ethic and the spirit of communism social class language game of oungan, manbo, gangan, and granmoun yo. Similarly, as the nation-state system in the West would come under the leadership of agents of the Protestant Ethic and the spirit of capitalism, the same holds true for kingship organizations of the African tribes and nations. Their kingship leadership and political culture emanated from their socioreligious life, i.e., the Vodou Ethic and the spirit of communism. During the Revolution, the African leadership was organized around their kingship and African military tactics, which was grounded in their religiosity (see Du Bois's Avengers of the New World, 2004, pgs. 108–109). It should also be mentioned that the majority of the early leaders were either oungan/manbo themselves or consulted with oungan yo and manbo yo.

3. My position here differs from Leslie G. Desmangles (1992) work, *The Faces of the Gods: Vodou and Roman Catholicism in Haiti*, which highlights the symbiotic nature of Vodou with Catholicism and Native American religions. Whereas Desmangles views Vodou as an "African-*derived* religion whose theological development has allowed its adherents not only to rekindle many of their African ethnic traditions, but to transform these traditions according to their environmental, sociocultural, and economic situations" (1992, pg. 172). I view Vodou as an African religion, a form of system and social integration, recursively reorganized and reproduced by the African people of Haiti as their practical consciousness amidst its transmogrifica-

tion by the power elites, i.e., oungan yo, manbo yo, gangan yo, and granmoun yo, of the system. So I accept Desmangles's notion of symbiosis, over syncretism, to highlight the evolution and reification of Vodou in parallel to Catholicism in Haiti, but I reject his idea that it became an African-derived religion. For me, Vodou is an African religion in which its power elites maintained and sustained in the face of persecution and oppression.

4. Many Haitians may utilize the Catholic/Protestant Ethic and the spirit of capitalism as their public face, and practice aspects (not its entire practical consciousness) of Vodou in secrecy. Others may solely practice one or the other. But the social structure was not reified as a syncretism of the two, which in turn interpellated and ounganified/manboified the masses as agents of the two via its ideological apparatuses. The two social structures emerged together, albeit the Catholic/Protestant Ethic and the spirit of capitalism had more power given its ideological apparatuses, i.e., army, police force, etc.

5. Genovese's work juxtaposes marronage in the colonies as the attempt of the Africans to restore their African modes of life against slavery, the "restorationist" movement, which stood against the "bourgeois-democratic wave" of the Age of Revolution. My work builds on this dichotomy in that I view the Affranchis goal in the revolutionary period of Haiti as being that of the latter, and the events of Bois Caiman and Jean-Jacques Dessalines's position as that of the former.

6. In the Vodou pantheon of 401 lwa yo, Jean-Jacques Dessalines is associated with Ogou Feray.

7. As heads of the Haitian nation state, Faustin Soulouque and Francois Duvalier, following Dessalines, openly, incorporated Vodou in their administrations and forms of governance.

Chapter One

Theorizing about the Constitution of Black Practical Consciousnesses in Haiti

At issue here is the origin and nature of consciousness and identity in general and black consciousness and identity in particular. Since the 1960s, there have been four similar schools of thought on understanding the origins and nature of black practical consciousnesses, the ideas blacks recursively reorganize and reproduce in their material practices, in the United States (US), the United Kingdom (UK), and the diaspora: the pathological-pathogenic and adaptive-vitality school in the US; and the anti-essentialist and anti-anti-essentialist schools in the UK and the diaspora. In the US, the pathological-pathogenic position suggests that in its divergences from white American norms and values black American practical consciousness is nothing more than a pathological form of, and reaction to, American consciousness rather than a dual (both African and American) hegemonic opposing "identity-in-differential" (the term is Gayatri Spivak's) to the American one (Elkins, 1959; Frazier, 1939,1957; Genovese, 1974; Murray, 1984; Moynihan, 1965; Myrdal, 1944; Wilson, 1978, 1987; Sowell, 1975, 1981; Stampp, 1956, 1971). Proponents of the adaptive-vitality school, building on the work of Melville J. Herskovits, suggest that the divergences are not pathologies but African "institutional transformations" preserved on the American landscape (Allen, 2001; Asante, 1988, 1990; Billingsley, 1968, 1970, 1993; Blassingame, 1972; Early, 1993; Gilroy, 1993; Gutman, 1976; Herskovits, 1958 [1941]; Holloway, 1990a; Karenga, 1993; Levine, 1977; Lewis, 1993; Lincoln and Mamiya, 1990; Nobles, 1987; Staples, 1978; Stack, 1974; Desmangles, 1992; West, 1993). Just the same in the UK and the diaspora, the two main opposing schools of thought are the anti-essentialist and the anti-anti-essentialist (Smith, 1960; Vera, 1960; Gilroy, 1993; Mercer, 1994; Clifford, 1997; Mocombe and Tomlin, 2010, 2013; Mocombe et al, 2014). Anti-essentialists as in the case of the US pathological-pathogenic school argue against any ideas of a black innate cultural phenomenon that unites all black people, and contends that diasporic identities and cultures cannot place African origin at the center of any attempt to understand the nature of black practical consciousnesses in the UK and the diaspora (Mercer, 1994, pg. 3). The anti-anti-essentialist position, in keeping with the logic of the adaptive-vitality school, posits, on the contrary, the idea that African memory retentions exist in diasporic cultures to some degree (Clifford, 1997, pg. 267–268). Contemporarily, all four positions have been criticized for either their structural determinism as in the case of the pathological-pathogenic and anti-essentialist approaches, or racial/cultural determinism as in the case of the adaptive-vitality and anti-anti-essentialist positions (Karenga, 1993; Reed, 1997; Gordon, 1999; Mocombe, 2008, 2012; Mocombe et al, 2014).

In directly or indirectly refuting these four positions for their structural and racial/cultural determinism, contemporary post-sixties and post-segregation era black scholars and critical race theorists, predominantly, in the United Kingdom (UK) and United States (US) attempt to understand black consciousnesses and communities by using post-structural, post-modern, and postcolonial theories to either reinterpret W.E.B. Du Bois's (1903) double consciousness construct as an epistemological mode of critical inquiry that characterizes the nature or essence of black consciousness, a la Cornel West (1993) and Paul Gilroy (1993); or, building on the social constructivist work of Frantz Fanon (1952 [2008]; 1963), offer an intersectional approach to the constitution of black consciousnesses and communities, which emphasizes the diverse and different levels of alienation, marginalization, and domination, class, race, gender, global location, age, and sexual identity, by which black consciousnesses and communities get constituted, a la bell hooks (1993) and Patricia Hill Collins (1990) (Reed, 1997; Gordon, 1999; Mocombe et al, 2014).[1] In spite of their efforts, these two dominant contemporary critical race theory responses to the pathological-pathogenic, adaptive-vitality, anti-essentialist, and anti-anti-essentialist positions inadequately resolve the structural and racial determinism of the aforementioned approaches by neglecting the fact that their theories and the practical consciousness of the theorists themselves derive from the class division and social relations of production of global capitalism or the contemporary capitalist world-system (Reed, 1997; Mocombe, 2008; Mocombe and Tomlin, 2012; Mocombe et al, 2014).

The former understanding, Du Boisian double consciousness, put forth by Paul Gilroy and Cornel West, with their emphasis on black improvisation as seen in Jazz and other black musical and religious forms, is not only problematic because it reiterates Du Bois's racial essentialism in constituting his notion of double consciousness (Reed, 1997; Mocombe, 2008). But the scholars are also mistaken because they assume their Cartesian, transcendental, intellectual activity, the epistemological mode of critical inquiry, in the academy as having ontological and epistemological status among the black masses in general in constituting their identity within and by the dialectical racial-class structure of global capitalist relations of production and its ideological apparatuses. In other words, instead of viewing their interpretation of Du Boisian double consciousness, as an epistemological mode of critical inquiry, as being a by-product of a Cartesian transcendental vantage point afforded to them by their academic training and bourgeois class positions as black professors seeking to define black consciousness along the social class language game of the white bourgeois lifestyles of the upper-class of owners and high-level executives as it stands against and in relation to black underclass bodies, material conditions, language, and ideology. Gilroy and West assume their interpretation of double consciousness as an epistemological mode of critical inquiry, which is similar to the negative dialectics of the Frankfurt School, to be how ontologically and epistemologically black people, whether in the US or the diaspora, in general come to constitute their practical consciousnesses within the modern state and the dialectic of the capitalist social structure of class inequality and differentiation of the West. In doing so, however, they neglect the fact that their conception, as was the case in W.E.B. Du Bois's conceptualization of double consciousness following the American Civil War, derives from the racial-class divisions of the American industrial/postindustrial capitalist social relations of production and its ideological apparatuses, which created two social (racial) class language games, a black bourgeois educated and professional class juxtaposed against the material conditions, practices, language, body, and ideology of a black underclass segregated in the ghettoes of Northern cities where industrial work was beginning to disappear to developing countries following the end of World War II. West and Gilroy, as Du Bois attempted to do for Southern agricultural black Americans following the Civil War, use double consciousness to highlight the contradictions of the society as encapsulated in, and revealed by, the material conditions of the black underclass of Northern cities in order to seek equality of opportunity, recognition, and distribution for them vis-à-vis whites and black bourgeois material conditions, bodies, language, etc. in a declining industrial social relations of production.

Just the same, the latter predominantly feminist position, conversely, building on the social constructivist position of Frantz Fanon, in refutation to the assumed hidden logic of heterosexual and patriarchal domination inherent in the theories of Du Bois, Gilroy, and West, attempts to offer an intersectional approach to the constitution of black consciousnesses, which emphasizes the different levels of domination, class, race, gender, global location, age, and sexual identity, by which black communities and consciousnesses get alienated, marginalized, and constituted. This post-structural, postmodern, postcolonial, and black feminist theorizing of bell hooks and Patricia Hill Collins, especially, epistemologically dismisses the dominant ontological status of the capitalist system/social structure by which the masses of blacks attempt to practically live out their lives for the theoretical assumptions of the indeterminacy of meaning and decentered subject of post-structural, post-modern, and postcolonial theorizing. They attempt to read back into the historical constitution of black identity and community life within and by the dialectic of a global capitalist social structure of racial class inequality the indeterminacy of meaning and decentered subject of post-structural, post-modern, postcolonial theorizing to highlight the variety of intersecting ways, race, class, age, sexual identity, etc., individual black subjects were and are alienated, marginalized, and dominated. As such, they commit the same bourgeois Cartesian transcendental intellectual fallacy that Gilroy and West do. Both hooks and Collins, from their transcendental vantage points, put the ontological status of the capitalist world-system, or "matrix of domination" to quote Collins, as reflected in the practices of the majority of blacks under erasure for the ontological and epistemological assumptions of post-modern and post-structural theorizing as though their bourgeois epistemological assumptions within a contemporary postindustrial capitalist social structure that attempts to reify and commodify individual identities for capital accumulation, is how all blacks, historically, initially encountered the matrix of domination and came to constitute their being-in-the-world within and by the global capitalist social structure of racial class inequality and differentiation. They fail to realize that intersectionality is a socio-political by-product of a postindustrial capitalist landscape or social structure seeking to decenter the bourgeois subject and allow a diversity of once discriminated against identities to emerge within the class division and social relations of postindustrial capitalist production so as to accumulate surplus-value by catering to the entertainment, financial, and service needs of these so-called new identities and their constructed class-based communities divided between a bourgeois class of blacks, homosexuals, transgenders, women, transsexuals, etc., "others," amongst the poor of their kind, seeking equality of opportunity, recognition, and distribution with whites (Mocombe, 2008, 2012; Fraser, 1994). Ambivalence, hybridity, liminality, créolité, négritude, etc., are the psychological processes, pathologies, and practical consciousness of the "other" bourgeoisies as they desire and struggle for equality of opportunity, recognition, and distribution with whites for themselves and members of the underclass of their fictive communities.

In other words, both positions because of their class origins and Cartesian ontological and epistemological (transcendental) activities and vantage points inadequately address the issue of how their intellectual assumptions and the practical consciousnesses in black communities within the global capitalist matrix of domination of the West historically and ontologically became constituted within and by the dialectical unfolding of racial-class divisions and social relations of production organized via mode of production, language, ideology, ideological apparatuses, and communicative discourse. They fail to synthesize their transcendental academic rhetoric with structural Marxist dialectics, which captures the racial-class divisions, ideological apparatuses, and the dialectical economic structure within which the practical consciousnesses of the black masses, the academic theories of hybridity, double consciousness, intersectionality, etc., and the identities of the theorists emerged.

I reject the postmodern, post-structural, and postcolonial emphasis on the decentered subject, intersectionality, ambiguity, hybridity, créolité, and liminality as the constituting basis of all subaltern or postcolonial identities. Again, the aforementioned are the psychological processes, pathologies, and practical consciousnesses of the "other" bourgeoisies and underclasses interpellated and embourgeoised by the ideology, ideological apparatuses, and modes of production of the West. As I see it, the decentered subject, ambiguity, hybridity, créolité, intersectionality, and liminality are relational concepts and processes socially and linguistically created by a structuring structure to interpellate human actors as such (Mocombe, 2012). In other words, they are concepts and processes created and used by the "other" bourgeoisies to highlight their psychology and practical consciousness in their quest for equality of opportunity, recognition, and distribution with whites. Whites of the contemporary post-industrial capitalist structuring structure in Europe and America in turn have co-opted and incorporated these processes, pathologies, and practical consciousnesses of the bourgeois other to interpellate and embourgeois human actors as hybrids, postcolonials, ambiguous identities, creoles, etc., in order to integrate them into the Protestant (postindustrial) capitalist world-system under American hegemony (Mocombe, 2012). The once discriminated against others, blacks, women, transgenders, homosexuals, etc., interpellated and embourgeoised by the modes of production, language, ideology, ideological apparatuses, and communicative discourse of Europe and America, internalize these, postindustrial, processes and concepts and recursively reorganize and reproduce them as their practical consciousness, in order to convict whites for not identifying with their ideas and ideals, as they (the "other") seek equality of opportunity, recognition, and distribution with their white counterparts as an "other" within the enframing ontology of the West under American hegemony.

Be that as it may, for me, consciousness and identity refers to (building on the structural Marxism of structuration theory grounded by a Weberian sociology as highlighted in his work, *The Protestant Ethic and the Spirit of Capitalism*) practical consciousness, the ideas and ideals, stemming from the language, communicative discourse, ideology, ideological apparatuses, and modes of production of a structuring structure, internalized and recursively (re) organized and reproduced in a material resource framework by human actors interpellated by other actors who control the resources of the framework (Mocombe, 2012, 2013, 2014, 2015).

Consciousness and identity defined as such, against the once prevailing view that Africans in the diaspora maintained their African traditions in the form of Africanisms during and after slavery this work argues the contrary (Allen, 2001; Asante, 1988, 1990; Billingsley, 1968, 1970, 1993; Blassingame, 1972; Early, 1993; Gilroy, 1993; Gutman, 1976; Herskovits, 1958 [1941]; Holloway, 1990a; Karenga, 1993; Levine, 1977; Lewis, 1993; Lincoln and Mamiya, 1990; Nobles, 1987; Staples, 1978; Stack, 1974; Desmangles, 1992; West, 1993). Outside of Haiti, the majority of black practical consciousnesses throughout the globe, contemporarily, are a dialectical by-product and differentiation of the Protestant Ethic and the spirit of capitalism of European societies. That is, interpellated, integrated, embourgeoised, and differentiated, via its languages, communicative discourse, modes of production, ideology, and ideological apparatuses, in the capitalist world-system following slavery and decolonization, the majority of black people in Africa and the African diaspora, contemporarily, internalize and recursively reorganize and reproduce a European way of life as black (other) agents of the Protestant Ethic and the spirit of capitalism seeking equality of opportunity, recognition, and distribution with their former white colonizers (Elkins, 1959; Frazier, 1939,1957; Genovese, 1974; Murray, 1984; Moynihan, 1965; Myrdal, 1944; Wilson, 1978, 1987, 1993; Sowell, 1975, 1981; Stampp, 1956, 1971).

In Africa and the black diaspora, an administrative bourgeoisie, interpellated, embourgeoised, and differentiated by the modes of production (agri-businesses, tourisms, manufacturing, call centers, industrial, postindustrial, etc.), languages (French, English, Spanish, Dutch, Portuguese, etc.), ideology (conservative, liberal, and radical Protestantism), ideological apparatuses (churches, schools, prisons, laws, the streets, etc.), and communicative discourse of their former white slavemasters and colonizers, emerged against a structurally differentiated underclass in poor material conditions who shared, due to the ideological apparatuses (schools, churches, prisons, urban street environments, police force, laws, etc.) and modes of production of slavery and the colonial system, in the ideology of their bourgeois counterparts whom they seek/sought to emulate. Hence amidst white racism, slavery, and colonialism, the majority of Africans, interpellated and embourgeoised by the language, mode of production, ideology, ideological apparatuses, and communicative discourse of their white masters internalized the ideas and ideals of the social system or structuring structure. They sought to recursively reorganize and reproduce these ideas and ideals as their practical consciousness for equality of opportunity, recognition, and distribution with whites by dialectically convicting European/white society for not identifying with their norms, values, and regulations, which the Africans, in a national position of their own, embody as an "other." Postmodern, post-structural, and postcolonial theorizing as encapsulated in the works of Aimé Césaire, Frantz Fanon, W.E.B. Du Bois, Stuart Hall, Paul Gilroy, Cornel West, Michael Eric Dyson, Patricia Hill-Collins, etc., captures and highlights the concepts, psychological processes, and pathologies of their desires and practical consciousness amidst white racism and discriminatory effects.

Like the rest of the black/African diaspora, in Haiti the administrative bourgeoisie, Affranchis, seeking equality of opportunity, recognition, and distribution with whites, would emerge and develop prior to, during, and following the Revolution. However, the majority of the Africans in the provinces and mountains of Haiti, as highlighted by Jacques Roumain and Jean Price-Mars, were not a structurally differentiated black other as one would find throughout Africa and the diaspora (I do recognize the minority of Africans—Santería, Candomblé, Obeah, etc.—in the Diaspora and Africa who attempt to maintain their Vodou Ethic and the spirit of communism but as in Haiti this is done against the practical consciousness of the administrative bourgeoisie in control of the state and the structurally differentiated others of their nation-states, which they attempt to interpellate and embourgeois). On the contrary, the majority of the Africans on the island maintained their African structuring structure, what I am calling here the Vodou Ethic and the spirit of communism social class language game, which they reified as the nature of reality as such via the language of Kreyol; the ideology of Vodou; its ideological apparatuses, i.e., lakous, peristyles, ounfo, *lwa yo*, herbal medicine, songs, dances, and zombification; and modes of production, i.e., *komes*, husbandry, and subsistence agriculture. Interpellated and ounganified/manboified by the ideological apparatuses of this structuring structure or social system, the African people of the island internalized and recursively reorganized and reproduced the ideas and ideals of the Vodou Ethic and the spirit of communism as their practical consciousness in the provinces and mountains under the leadership of *oungan yo, manbo yo, gangan yo/dokté fey*, and *granmoun yo* against the practical consciousness of agents (Affranchis) of the Catholic/Protestant Ethic and the spirit of capitalism who controlled the state, its language, ideology, ideological apparatuses, and communicative discourse at the expense of the control of the material resource framework and the mode of production, which the Africans controlled and dominated.

In other words, two social systems or structuring structures representing the nature of reality as such emerged on the island following the revolution, the Vodou Ethic and the spirit of communism social class language game of the Africans and the Catholic/Protestant Ethic and spirit of capitalism social class language game of the mulatto elites and petit-bourgeois free blacks.

The originating moments of the Haitian Revolution as initiated on August 14th, 1791 at Bois Caïman by Boukman Dutty, Cecile Fatiman, and Edaïse was led by Africans under the leadership of *oungan yo, manbo yo, gangan yo/dokté fey*, and *granmoun yo* anti-dialectically, seeking to constitute and recursively (re) organize and reproduce their African Kreyol and Vodou practical-consciousness, the Vodou Ethic and the spirit of communism social class language game, in the world via the ideology of Vodou; its ideological apparatuses, i.e., lakous, peristyles, *lwa yo*, herbal medicine, proverbs, songs, dances, musical instruments, ounfo, and secret societies; and modes of production, subsistence agriculture, husbandry, and komes. This latter worldview (form of system and social integration) stood against the bourgeois Catholic/Protestant liberalism of whites, the mulatto elites and petit-bourgeois free blacks or Affranchis class of Haiti, who would subsequently, with the assassination of the *oungan,* Vodou priest, Jean-Jacques Dessalines on October 17th, 1806, undermine that attempt for a more dialectical liberal purposive-rationale, similar to the rest of the black/African diaspora. The latter's, Affranchis, failure to *effectively* enforce and establish ideological apparatuses in the provinces and the mountains to interpellate, embourgeois, and differentiate the masses as agents of the Catholic/Protestant Ethic and the spirit of capitalism against the mode of production, ideology, ideological apparatuses, and communicative discourse of the Vodou Ethic and the spirit of communism of *oungan yo, manbo yo,* and *granmoun yo* undermined their attempt, however. Albeit they would subsequently work with foreign white merchants to underdeveloped the provinces and mountains by undermining the subsistence agricultural, husbandry, and *komes* of the Africans through taxation, importation of cheap foreign goods, and silencing their history and historical narratives through the hybridity, créolité, négritude, etc., logic of postmodern, post-structural, and postcolonial theories as embedded in the works of Frantz Fanon, Aimé Césaire, and Léopold Sédar Senghor, among many others (Trouillot, 1990, 1995; Du Bois, 2012; Ramsey, 2014).

It is this initial divergent path against slavery and liberal bourgeois Protestantism that would come to constitute the identity of the Haitian masses under the leadership of *oungan yo, manbo yo, gangan yo/dokté fey*, and *granmoun yo*, and sets the originating moments of the Haitian Revolution and Haitian practical consciousness apart, as a distinct anti-dialectical phenomenon, from the dialectical desires and purposive-rationale of an elite liberal hybrid group, the mulatto and black petit-bourgeois elites in Haiti and liberal black Protestant bourgeois males of America and elsewhere in the diaspora. The latter two sought and seek to serve as the bearers of ideological and linguistic domination for the black masses in both countries, respectively, by dialectically recursively reorganizing and reproducing the agential moments of their former white slavemasters and colonizers—for equality of opportunity, recognition, and distribution—via the state and its ideological apparatuses as opposed to reconstituting their being-in-the-world from an African worldview as the Haitian/African maroons did in establishing the counter-plantation system via the language, communicative discourse, ideology, ideological apparatuses, and modes of production of their Vodou Ethic and the spirit of communism social class language game.

Hence, against contemporary postmodern, post-structural, and postcolonial theories, I am not suggesting that the Africans of Haiti syncretized the Africanism of their African Vodou practical consciousness with that of the Europeans, and the ambiguity, hybridity, créolité, and liminality of that syncretism provided them the space to speak as subalterns. On the contrary, at Bois Caiman, the Africans rejected the European worldview and *oungan yo, manbo yo, bokor yo, gangan yo/dokté fey*, and *granmoun yo* (elders) syncretized their African worldviews with native Taino traditions, which paralleled the African. They reified and sought to institutionalize it in the material world via ideological apparatuses, Lakous, peristyles, herbal medicine, *lwa yo*, and proverbs used to interpellate and ounganify/manboify the African masses against that of the European worldview or language game of the Affranchis. Créolité, hybridity, intersectionality, ambivalence, liberal bourgeois Protestantism, etc., is the practical consciousness of the Affranchis and the structurally differentiated black others interpellated and embourgeoised by the ideologies, ideological apparatuses, and modes of production of their former white and black colonial slavemasters amidst their continual experiences of racism and discrimination as they seek equality of opportunity, recognition, and distribution.

To sum up, whereas Haitians, sixty-seven percent were directly from Africa when the Revolution commenced, because of their early freedom from slavery and white colonial rule were able to maintain their African material practices and consciousnesses which they synthesized with Taino practices and reified via the ideology of Vodou, ideological apparatuses such as lakous, peristyles, subsistence agricultural mode of production, husbandry, and *komes* under the leadership of *oungan yo, manbo yo,* and *granmoun yo.* The petit-bourgeois blacks and mulatto elites, Affranchis, like their African, black American, and diasporic counterparts for example, given their interpellation, differentiation, and embourgeoisement via the mode of production, language, ideology, ideological apparatuses, and communicative discourse of the West, sought to dialectically adopt the Catholic/Protestant Ethic and spirit of capitalism of their former European colonizers (as a Francophile neocolonial oligarchy) by which to constitute the nation-state of Haiti. Unlike the other black administrative bourgeoisies in America and the diaspora, however, the Affranchis did not encounter a structurally differentiated black other in the provinces and mountains. They encountered an African people with their own structuring structure (form of system and social integration), i.e., language, communicative discourse, mode of production, ideology, and ideological apparatuses. As such, the Affranchis, like their white counterparts, attempted to, via racism, slavery, and colonization, recolonize the African people of the island. It is their, Affranchis, attempt, as a Francophile neocolonial oligarchy, to convert the Africans, by undermining their history, historical narratives, language, ideology, ideological apparatuses, communicative discourse, and modes of production, into a structurally differentiated black other, i.e., masses, peasant class, laborers, creoles, hybrids, etc., within the capitalist world-system under American hegemony, which have led to the misery and poverty of Haiti and the Haitian people. As previously highlighted, the Africans,

> [t]ook over the land they had once worked as slaves, creating small farms where they raised livestock and grew crops to feed themselves and sell in local markets. On these small farms, they did all the things that had been denied to them under slavery: they built families, practiced their religion, and worked for themselves.... Haiti's rural population effectively undid the plantation model. By combining subsistence agriculture with the production of some crops for export, [*komes,*] they created a system that guaranteed them a better life, materially and socially, than that available to most other people of African descent in the Americas throughout the nineteenth and early twentieth centuries. But they did not succeed in establishing that system in the country as a whole. In the face of most Haitians' unwillingness to work the plantations, Haiti's ruling groups retreated but did not surrender. Ceding, to some extent, control of the land, they took charge of the ports and the export trade. And they took control of the state, heavily taxing the goods produced by the small-scale farmers and thereby reinforcing the economic divisions between the haves and the have-nots (Du Bois, 2012, pg. 6).

Hence, the Affranchis, following the Revolution, did not reproduce and enforce the ideological apparatuses of the West throughout the island to interpellate, embourgeois, and differentiate the masses as agents of the Catholic/Protestant Ethic and the spirit of capitalism as was done throughout Africa and the diaspora by whites and the black administrative bourgeoisies who would replace them following slavery and decolonization. Instead, they sought their interpellation, embourgeoisement, and differentiation by silencing their history, historical narratives, and subverting their komes, husbandry, and subsistence agriculture for those, i.e., agribusinesses, manufacturing, and tourism, of the West in order to build their (Affranchis) own wealth and payback the independence debt to France at the expense of the well-being of the African masses and the country. Haiti's contemporary milieu of poverty and political instability is a result of the continual struggle between those, agents of the Catholic/Protestant Ethic and the spirit of capitalism, seeking to reproduce it as a simulacrum of the West, a periphery state (the Taiwan of the Caribbean) within the capitalist world-system under American hegemony, and those, agents of the Vodou Ethic and the spirit of communism, seeking to constitute it as sovereign state where the resources are shared democratically and equitably amongst its citizens.

Within Mocombe's (2014, 2015) phenomenological structuralism, this work, against contemporary postmodern, post-structural, and postcolonial theories, seeks to offer a dialectical understanding of the constitution of a *minority* of Haitian life within the class division and social relations of production of the global Protestant capitalist world-system, which distinguishes it from an anti-dialectical reading of the originating moments of the Haitian Revolution and the constitution of the identity of the majority of the people in the provinces, mountains, and urban slums on the island, which stood and stands against it. I go on to demonstrate how at the heart of Haiti's poverty is this struggle between these two opposing structuring structures and practical-consciousnesses, the Catholic/Protestant Ethic and the spirit of capitalism social class language game of the mulatto elites and petit-bourgeois blacks, i.e., *Affranchis*, on the one hand, reified via the French language, ideology of the Republican state, neoliberal capitalism, mode of production, i.e., agribusiness, tourism, and textile industry, and its ideological apparatuses; and the Vodou Ethic and spirit of communism social class language game of the masses, with its own history, language (Kreyol), mode of production (subsistence agriculture and *komes*), ideology, Vodou, and ideological apparatuses, lakous, peristyles, ounfo, etc., under the leadership of *oungan yo, manbo yo, gangan yo/dokté fey*, and *granmoun yo*, on the other.

NOTE

1. Lewis R. Gordon (1999) in his short essay, "A Short History of the Critical in Critical Race Theory," traces two strands as to the origins of the "critical" basis of CRT. The first strand builds on the theoretical discourse of W.E.B. Du Bois (1903), and the second on the works of Frantz Fanon. From Du Bois many critical race theorists (Derrick Bell, Lucius T. Outlaw, Tommy Lott, Robert Gooding-Williams, and Josiah Young) adopt his distinction between identity and policy to constitute their eliminative discourses for racial equality within the liberal democratic state. The Fanonian School (Cornel West, Paul Gilroy, David Goldberg, Michael Omi, Howard Winant, Anthony Appiah, Naomi Zack, Charles Mills, Stuart Hall, Victor Anderson, and many others) represents the postmodern and post-structural strand of CRT, and highlights the constructivity of racial formation. That is, like Fanon, "they bring into focus the tension between structural identities and lived identities and the tension between constitutional theories and raw environmental appeals" to highlight the racism, sexism, etc., by which the West constitute itself against blacks, women, homosexuals, etc., as they experience the material resource framework in their everyday lives (Gordon, 1999). Gordon, goes on to highlight how the latter school is further divided into two camps: those (Anthony Appiah, Naomi Zack, Charles Mills, and Victor Anderson) who hold on to the idea that liberalism can resolve the racial issues and tensions; and those (Cornel West, for example) who are more radical and have lost faith in the ideals of liberalism to resolve them. In either case, both positions represent a fight against the power elites of the West for equality of opportunity, recognition, and distribution within its "enframing" logic of organizing and reproducing the material resource framework, not for an alternative constructed identity to it (Fraser, 1994). In other words, critical race theorists are seeking pluralism within the enframing ontology and praxis of the West, i.e., racial "other" agents of the Protestant Ethic and the spirit of capitalism,

not to replace that ontology and epistemology with an alternative practical consciousness upon which to reorganize and reproduce the material resource framework. The reason for this is because the theorists are themselves Westerners and are seeking to dialectically convict the society of not identifying with its values and ideals even though those very values and ideals, which they recursively reorganize and reproduce in their own praxis, threaten humanity and the earth with its consumerist, exploitative, and accumulative logic of organizing the material resource framework. Hence CRT, regardless of its strands, is not critical enough because of its identitarian, dialectical, logic, which is grounded in the negative dialectic of the Frankfurt school, which is not an anti-dialectical logic or constructive identity which opposes the West as one finds in the Vodou Ethic and the spirit of communism of the originating moments of the Haitian Revolution at Bois Caiman and the contemporary Islamic Fundamentalist movements of the Middle East, for examples. The latter, anti-dialectical logics offer alternative means or constructivity of organizing the material resource framework we call the earth in order to structure lived-experiences around an alternative means of existence, is necessary if humanity is to survive the consumerist, exploitative, and accumulative logic of the West as it threatens the earth and all life on it. Critical Race Theorists are unable to offer that anti-dialectical response because of their incessant claim for equality of opportunity, recognition, and distribution within the already existing liberal bourgeois Protestant constructed identity by which the state and their identities are constituted. Albeit, Cornel West's recent attack against the American and global oligarchs of the capitalist world-system is an attempt to offer that anti-dialectical response. However, given his Western identity, he does not offer a prescription, outside of Jazz improvisation, of what that new "new world order" and its practical consciousness or constructed identity should look like (as one finds in the counter-hegemonic plantation system of Haitian Vodou) if we and the planet will survive in the near future. The Vodou Ethic and the spirit of communism of the Haitian Revolution I argue here offer such an anti-dialectical discourse and discursive practice to the Protestant Ethic and the spirit of capitalism of the West and CRT.

Chapter Two

Phenomenological Structuralism

Against the Hegelian dialectical, postmodern, post-structural, and postcolonial logic of many white Western and black bourgeois scholars exploring the
Haitian Revolution, culture, and identity of the Haitian people, I propose an
anti-dialectical perspective grounded in the Weberian (1958 [1904–1905])
sociology of *The Protestant Ethic and the spirit of capitalism* coupled with
the structural Marxism of structuration theory.[1] From the former my phenomenological structural sociology borrows the logic of the internalization of
the ideas and ideals of the ideological superstructure of a society as the basis
by which social actors go about recursively reorganizing and reproducing
their being-in-the-world as their purposive-rationality or practical consciousness, which is the language of the latter, structurationism. Phenomenological
structuralism seeks to fix structurationism to account for alternative agential
moments outside of structural reproduction and differentiation. In the end, I
apply my structurationist sociology to understanding the constitution of Haitian practical consciousness as the parallel development of two forms of
system and social integration, the Catholic/Protestant Ethic and the spirit of
capitalism of the whites and Affranchis on the one hand; and the Vodou
Ethic and the spirit of communism of the majority of the Africans on the
other.

BACKGROUND

The structurationist or praxis school in the social sciences is commonly associated with Jürgen Habermas (1987 [1981], 1984 [1981]), Pierre Bourdieu
(1990 [1980], 1984), and Anthony Giddens (1984) in sociology, and Marshall Sahlins (1976, 1995 [1981]) in anthropology (Crothers, 2003; Ortner,
1984). Elaborated in a series of theoretical works and empirical studies,

structurationists or praxis theorists account for agency and consciousness in social structure or system, "by clamping action and structure together in a notion of 'practice' or 'practises'" (Crothers, 2003, pg. 3). That is, structures are not only external to social actors, as in the classic structural functional view, but are also internal rules and resources produced and reproduced by actors "unconsciously" (intuitively) in their practices. In structurationist or praxis theory, as Marx one-hundred years before suggested, the structure is "not a substantially separable order of reality", but "simply the 'ideal' form in which the totality of 'material' relations...are manifested to conscious-ness..." (Sayer, 1987, pg. 84). From this perspective, accordingly, structure or, sociological speaking, social structure, "may set [(ideological)] condi-tions to the historical process, but it is dissolved and reformulated in material practice [(through mode of production and ideological apparatuses)], so that history becomes the realization, in the form of society, of the actual [(embod-ied rules)] resources people put into play" (Sahlins, 1995 [1981], pg. 7): consciousness, as a result, refers to "practical consciousness" or the dissolu-tion and reformulation of a social structure's terms (norms, values, prescrip-tions, and proscriptions) in material practice.

Although this Neo-Marxist "clamping together" of structure, praxis, and consciousness descriptively accounts for "the individual moment of phenom-enology" by explaining the unanimity, closure, and "intentionality" of a form of human action or sociation, the capitalist social (material) relations of production and its class division, which constitutes the integrative actions of modern society. It fails, however, as pointed out in the epistemological post-modern/post-structural positions of Michel Foucault, Jacques Derrida, Jacques Lacan, bell hooks, and Patricia Hill-Collins, to account for the ori-gins and nature of fully visible alternative forms of practices (i.e., "the vari-ability of the individual *moments* of phenomenology") within the dominant order that are not class based, but are the product of the deferment of mean-ing in ego-centered communicative discourse, a la the Vodou Ethic and the spirit of communism social class language game of the Vodou leadership of Haiti. Structurationists fail to see that society and its dominant institutional-ized identity and behavior is not solely "one-dimensional," i.e., a duality, and differentiated by the dialectic of capitalist social relations of production, but is constituted, through power relations, as transition, relation, and difference. This difference, akin to Jacques Derrida's *différance*, is not biologically (ra-cially) hardwired in the social actor. It is a result of self-reflective and non-impulsive social actors, upon internalizing the arbitrary structural terms or signifiers of their society via their consciousness, bodies, language, and lin-guistic communication, conceiving of and exercising other forms of being-in-the-world from that of the dominant symbolic order and its structural differentiation or relational logic through the deferment of meaning in ego-centered communicative discourse (Habermas, 1987 [1981], 1984 [1981]; Giddens, 1984).

By "clamping" action, structure, and consciousness together, i.e., part/ whole totality, however, structurationists do not account for, nor demonstrate, the nature and relation of this non-biologically and non-impulsive determined difference (*différance*) to that of the dominant practices of the social structure as highlighted in the theorizing of postmodern and poststructural scholars. Instead, they re-introduce the problem in a new form: How do we know or *exercise* anything at odds with an embodied received view grounded in, and differentiated by, capitalist social relations of production? Paul C. Mocombe's (2013, 2014, 2015) phenomenological structural ontology, phenomenological structuralism, seeks to fix structurationism to account for this problematic by synthesizing the materialism of physics, with the agential initiatives highlighted in the phenomenological method and discourses of Husserl, Heidegger, Merleau-Ponty, and Sartre, the Neo-Marxist structuralism of structurationism, and Wittgenstein's notion of language game. For Mocombe, in building on the duality concept of structuration theory, human social action, consciousness, and identity is not only a duality determined by their relation to the mode of production and its differentiation. But it is also a dualism, the externalized structure of a society reified, in the words of Louis Althusser (1970, 2001), through language, ideology, ideological apparatuses, communicative discourse, and the mode of production. As such, social action and identity/consciousness constitution are not necessarily a duality, i.e., the internalization of the external language, ideology, etc., of a social structure recursively (re) organized and reproduced as the practical consciousness of a social actor. Duality is a contingent phenomenon based on a human subject's stance vis-à-vis the reified structure, which presupposes their existence and the will of those in power positions. In other words, alternative actions or practical consciousnesses are distinct reified languages, ideologies, ideological apparatuses, and modes of production from that of the dominant social structure within which they operate. These alternative actions or practical consciousnesses are the product of four sources, and Being's stance, ready-to-hand, unready-to-hand, and present-at-hand, vis-à-vis them: 1) the drives of the body and brain, 2) impulses of residual actions/ memories of embodied recycled past consciousnesses of subatomic particles, 3) ideologies of a social system along with its differentiating logic (structural reproduction and differentiation), which produces the variability of actions and practices in cultures, social structures, or social systems as highlighted by structurationist theorists, and 4) the "present-at-hand" phenomenological meditation/deferment that occurs on the latter actions via linguistic/symbolic communication. The exercise of power by social actors in power positions in the ideological apparatuses social actors are interpellated in, in the end, determines what practical consciousnesses are allowed to manifest in a material resource framework without a social actor facing alienation, marginalization, or death.

To this end of fixing structurationism to account for the nature and origins of alternative practical consciousnesses outside the structural reproduction and differentiation of capitalist relations of production, Paul C. Mocombe's (2014, 2015) phenomenological structuralism builds on the material relationship highlighted in physics between the identity and indeterminate behavior of subatomic particles highlighted in quantum mechanics and the determinate behavior of atomic particles in their aggregation as highlighted in general relativity to understand the material constitution of consciousness at the subatomic/neuronal level in, and as, the brain and its manifestation as human practical consciousness at the atomic level as revealed by modes of production, language, ideologies, ideological apparatuses, communicative discourse, and the actions of the body. I go on, in the subsequent chapters, to utilize Mocombe's structurationism, phenomenological structural ontology, to account for the emergence of the two worldviews (forms of system and social integration), the Catholic/Protestant Ethic and the spirit of capitalism social class language game and the Vodou Ethic and the spirit of communism social class language game, found in the nation-state of Ayiti (Haiti).

THEORY

According to the tenets of quantum physics as reflected in supersymmetry theory, dark matter, parallel universes (multiverses), and the EPR paradox, the universe is composed of ordinary matter (atoms and molecules) and dark matter (axions, wimps, neutrinos, bosons, and fermions).[2] Dark matter, as opposed to ordinary matter, constitutes over eighty percent of the material substance that constitute the cosmos. This dark matter is not constituted by atoms and molecules like ordinary matter but consists of subatomic particles and energy. The particles in the nature of quarks are identified as wimps or axions, very tiny particles that contribute to the formation of nuclear components. These tiny particles are conceived of as coiled energies, strings of space-time, packets of energy-like photons. They are physical in nature but immaterial, and coexist, in a parallel/alternate universe, with ordinary matter in the same location without impediment or interference. They belong to the fermion family of invisible particles whose counterparts are named a boson, which is pure energy. So, as highlighted in supersymmetry theory, for every boson particle of matter, a symmetry counterpart, fermion, exists which manifests itself as force or energy. Thus, for every reality we discover in the solid world around us, we must assume that there exists a symmetric counterpart, or boson, which is invisible but is nevertheless as physical as its visible counterpart. These supersymmetric doubles constitute the backbone of alternate realities, parallel universes that are displayed in ten dimensions, including our ordinary three-dimensional Cartesian reality. Moreover, according to the EPR paradox, these particles have psychic properties. That is, the particles are conscious. They are aware of their position, of themselves, and of their surroundings. In other words, the multiverses created by these particles are endowed with consciousness.

Hence the multiverse originated either by fiat or quantum fluctuation. It is a bosonic force that was brought forth together with a fermion counterpart. It is also the primeval pan-psychic field whose fermion can be called a psychion, a particle of consciousness. These have evolved together to produce the four forces of nature, electromagnetic force; gravity; the strong nuclear force; and weak nuclear force, in our universe, which in turn produced atoms, molecules, and aggregated life. In other words, according to quantum mechanics subatomic particles of energy constitute all the matter of the universe via the Higgs Boson Field, i.e., the god particle, which objectifies and materialize the matter that we are, see, hear, taste, feel, and touch. Subatomic particles constitute our material bodies and consciousness as neuronal energies, which constitute and operate the brain and the body. However, subatomic matter, which are strings at the subatomic particle level, operate differently from observable objectified energy, matter, in that their behavior are indeterminate and can exist in multiple places, dimensions or parallel universes, simultaneously prior to being observed or even during observation as aggregated matter. In fact, the subatomic particles that constitute our material bodies and consciousness as neuronal energies are the same subatomic particles that constitute everything that we consider to be the world, universe, other species, etc. At the subatomic particle level we are not subjects contemplating an object, i.e., the world, multiverse, etc., we are the world, an undifferentiating energy. Hence, the implication suggested by the Standard Model of physics is that the observable and non-observable matter that constitutes our universe exists elsewhere in other unseen dimensions and parallel universes simultaneously with our own dispensation of space-time. Contrary to the Copenhagen interpretation of quantum mechanics, we do not occupy a universe. We are part of a multiverse with a plethora of I (s) and other sentient beings existing in them indistinguishable from one another at the subatomic level as energy. They become distinguishable at the atomic level through subatomic particle aggregation, i.e., matter. Subatomic particles aggregate to form objectified matter, universes, worlds, species and sentient beings with consciousness, etc. The plethora of I (s) and other sentient beings are constituted and connected via subatomic particles that are recycled throughout and as the multiverse to constitute and operate consciousness as subatomic neuronal energies of the body and the brain, which encounters objectified matter as objectified matter via the actions and senses of the brain, body, language, ideologies, ideological apparatuses, modes of

production, and communicative discourse. In essence, consciousness is recycled subatomic energies of the multiverse objectified and embodied, similar
to Hegel's conceptualization of *Geist*. Whereas for Hegel *Geist* is distinct
from the material world and unfolds dialectically in it, via embodiment of
certain individuals, towards an ever-increasing rationalization of the world
towards self-knowledge and freedom. For me the historical manifestation,
Being-in-Spacetime, of the objectification of subatomic particles of the universe as consciousnesses and bodies has no definitive end-goal and is indeterminate. But constrained in materialized space-time by our material bodies
and power relations or the social class language games, dualism, of those
whose objectification, i.e., historicity, precedes our own individual consciousnesses and control the economic conditions of a material resource
framework, which they reify via mode of production, language, ideologies,
ideological apparatuses, and communicative discourse.

Like the laws of physics, which attempt to regulate and determine subatomic particle activity as general law (Theory of general relativity) once
they are aggregated, the social class language game of those who control the
economic conditions of a material resource framework attempts to regulate
and determine the indeterminacy of meaning unfolding in and as the consciousnesses of social actors via bodies, mode of production, language, ideology, ideological apparatuses, and communicative discourse. Unlike, postmodern and post-structural theorizing, which utilize the indeterminacy of
meaning as highlighted by the unconscious in the psychoanalytic works of
Sigmund Freud and Jacques Lacan, my phenomenological structuralism
analogously builds on the material relationship in physics between the identity and indeterminate behavior of subatomic particles highlighted in quantum mechanics and the determinate behavior of atomic particles in their
aggregation as highlighted in general relativity to understand the material
constitution of consciousnesses at the subatomic/neuronal level in, and as,
the brain and their manifestation as human practical consciousnesses, via the
body, at the atomic level. I do not, unlike psychoanalysts like Lacan and
Freud or phenomenologists like Edmund Husserl, claim to know how the
embodiment of recycled subatomic neuronal energies via the microtubules of
the brain come to constitute consciousnesses in the brain and their subsequent revelation as the practical consciousnesses of bodies. That is, the
transcendental ego or I of a differentiated individual subject, which I or
anyone else does not have access to, could just as much be the past I, recycled subatomic particles, of a sentient being from an alternative universe or
dimension of the multiverse and not necessarily the product of repression and
the rule of the father, i.e., social construction. Psychoanalysis and the indeterminacy of the processes of the unconscious and the universal mapping of
consciousnesses, i.e., its form of understanding, by Edmund Husserl's
transcendental phenomenology and contemporary neuroscientists, for me, in

other words, neither adequately captures the indeterminate behavior of embodied recycled subatomic particles as neuronal energies of the brain and the myriad of practical consciousnesses they may produce as revealed by diverse practices of bodies, nor can they account for the origins of the transcendental ego or I. Husserl, Freud, and contemporary neuroscientists attempt to highlight and capture the Kantian form of the understanding and sensibilities of the aggregated body and brain, which is unable to explain how aggregated subatomic quantum particles give rise to the transcendental ego of consciousness, which produces praxis. I am not claiming that my phenomenological structural ontology captures this process. The only thing of consciousness, produced by embodied subatomic particles, I am claiming to be ontogenetically universal is the stance of the transcendental ego, what Heidegger calls the *analytic of Dasein*, vis-à-vis the drives of the aggregated body, impulses of recycled past consciousnesses of subatomic particle energies, language, ideology, ideological apparatuses, structural reproduction and differentiation, once it becomes constituted by subatomic particles. Hence my use of phenomenology in phenomenological structuralism. I hold on to the phenomenological logic of Husserl, Heidegger, Merleau-Ponty, and Sartre here to capture, in a behavioral sense, the how, via Heidegger's three stances ready-to-hand, unready-to-hand, present-at-hand, of identity constitution amidst indeterminacy of consciousnesses and actions produced by embodied recycled subatomic neuronal energies/particles.

It is the stance of a transcendental ego vis-à-vis 1) the drives of the aggregated body, 2) the drives or impulses of recycled subatomic particles, 3) structural reproduction and differentiation of ideologies, ideological apparatuses, and mode of production, and 4) the deferment of meaning in ego-centered communicative discourse, which determines our practical consciousness. In other words, what I am suggesting here in my phenomenological structuralism, which seeks to highlight the phenomenology of being-in-the-structure-of-those-who-control-a-material-resource-framework and the origins of our practical consciousness, is that embodiment is the objectification of the transcendental ego, which is a part of an universal *élan vital* (Henri Bergson's term), the primeval pan-psychic field, that has ontological status in dimensions existing at the subatomic particle level and gets embodied via, and as, the body and connectum of Being's brains. Hence the transcendental ego is the universal *élan vital*, which is the neuronal energies of past, present, and future Beings-of-the-multiverse, embodied. This transcendental ego, and its stance, encounters a material world via and as the body and brain in mode of production, language, ideology, ideological apparatuses, and communicative discourse.

Once embodied in and as human individual consciousnesses in a particular universe, world, and historical social formation, the transcendental ego becomes an embodied hermeneutic structure that never encounters the world and the things of the world in themselves via the aggregated built-in genetic ontology of the body and the impulses of the neuronal energies. Instead embodied hermeneutic individual consciousness is constituted via the recycled subatomic neuronal particle energies which are aggregated as a transcendental ego and the body in their encounter and interpretation of past recycled neuronal memories and things enframed in and by the language, bodies, ideology, ideological apparatuses, practices, and communicative discourses of those who control the economic conditions of a material resource framework and its social relations of production. In consciousness, as phenomenology posits, it (individual subjective consciousness of embodied beings) can either choose to accept the structural knowledge, differentiation, and practices of the body; the impulses of recycled past consciousnesses of subatomic neuronal particles; the ideologies of those who control, via their bodies, mode of production, language, ideology, ideological apparatuses, and communicative discourse, the economic conditions of the material resource framework and recursively reorganize and reproduce them in their practices; or reject them, given the ability to defer meaning in ego-centered communicative discourse, for an indeterminate amount of action-theoretic ways-of-being-in-the-world-with-others, which they may assume at the threat to their ontological security. It is Being's stance, ready-to-hand, unready-to-hand, and present-at-hand vis-à-vis 1) the drives of the body, 2) impulses of residual actions/memories of embodied recycled past consciousnesses, 3) the phenomenological meditation/deferment that occurs on the latter actions via linguistic communication, and 4) ideologies of a social system along with its differentiating logic, coupled with the will of those in power positions, which produces the variability of actions and practices in cultures, social structures, or social systems that enframe the material world.

As such, as in Heidegger's phenomenology, phenomenology in phenomenological structuralism is not just transcendental, it is also hermeneutical. The act of interpretation (based on the stance of Being) or an embodied hermeneutic structure via the body, language, ideology, and communicative discourse is a universal precondition of being-in-the-world-with-other-human-beings. However, whereas Heidegger is interested in the question of the meaning of Being-as-such, i.e., the phenomenology of Being, phenomenological structuralism is concerned with the *sociology of Being*, the question of the meaning or constitutive nature of embodied Being-as-such's-being-in-the-world-with-others who attempt to constrain practical consciousnesses via their bodies, language, ideologies, ideological apparatuses, and communicative discourse derived from social relations of production. That is, as in Martin Heidegger's phenomenological ontology, I am interested in the necessary societal relationship and practical consciousnesses that emerge out of the phenomenology of Being-in-the-world-within-structures-of-signification-of-others, who control the economic conditions of the material resource framework we find ourselves existing in, that presuppose our historicity, and Being's perceptions, responses, and practices, i.e., relations, to these structures-of-signification in order to be in the world. Unlike Heidegger, however, my concern is not with the phenomenology of being-in-the-world as such because Being never encounters the world and its transcendental ego as the-thing-itself. Instead being encounters the world via its body/brain, recycled (impulses of) past consciousnesses, and structures of signification, which derive from class division and social relations of production as reified in the bodies (as agential initiative), language, ideology, ideological apparatuses, and communicative discourse of those who control the resources of a material resource framework.

Be that as it may, whereas I accept the Husserlian phenomenological understanding that the facts of the world and their conditions of possibility are present in consciousness, i.e., the notion of intentionality, consciousness is always consciousness of something as we experience being-in-the-world-with-other-beings via our consciousness, i.e., transcendental ego, bodies, language, ideologies, and communicative discourse. My position here, however, is that as an embodied hermeneutic structured being we never experience the facts of the world and their conditions of possibility as the "the things in themselves." We experience them not culturally and historically, which is a present-at-hand viewpoint, but structurally and relationally, via the bodies, language, ideology, and communicative discourse in institutions or ideological apparatuses, i.e., the social class language game, of those who control the economic conditions of the material resource framework we find ourselves thrown-in, via our bodies, language, and communicative discourse. In other words, my phenomenology of embodied Being-in-the-world-as-such's-Being-with-others, phenomenological structuralism, synthesizes Merleau-Ponty's and Heidegger's phenomenology with Karl Marx's materialism and Ludwig Wittgenstein's language game to suggest that being-in-the-world with others, our practical consciousness, is a product of our interpretation, acceptance, or rejection of the symbols of signification, social class language game, of those bodies in institutional/ideological power positions who control via their bodies, language, ideologies, ideological apparatuses, and communicative discourse the economic conditions of a material resource framework as we encounter them and their symbols/signifiers in institutions or ideological apparatuses via our own transcendental ego, bodies, language, and communicative discourse. Hence we never experience the things-in-themselves of the world culturally and historically in consciousness. We experience them structurally or relationally, and our stances, ready-to-hand, unready-to-hand, present-at-hand, vis-à-vis these ideological structures determine our practical consciousness or behaviors.

We initially know, experience, and utilize the things of the world in the preontological ready-to-hand mode, which is structural and relational. That is, our bodies and impulses encounter, know, experience, and utilize the things of the world in consciousness, intersubjectively, via their representation as objects of knowledge, truth, usage, and experience enframed and defined in the relational logic and practices or language game (Wittgenstein's term) of the institutions or ideological apparatuses of the other beings-of-the-material resource framework whose historicity comes before our own and gets reified in and as language, ideology, ideological apparatuses, and communicative discourse based on their mode of production or satisfying the needs of the aggregated body. This is the predefined phenomenal structural, i.e., ontological, world we, the psychion or transcendental ego of the primeval pan-psychic field, and our bodies are thrown-in in coming to be-in-the-world. How an embodied-hermeneutically-structured Being as such solipsistically goes on to view, experience, understand, and utilize the predefined objects of knowledge, truth, and experienced defined by others and their conditions of possibilities in consciousness in order to formulate their practical consciousness is albeit indeterminate. Heidegger is accurate, however, in suggesting that three stances or modes of encounter (Analytic of Dasein), "presence-at-hand," "readiness-to-hand," and "un-readiness-to-hand," characterizes our views of the things of consciousness represented intersubjectively via bodies, language, ideology, and communicative discourse, and subsequently determine our practical consciousness or social agency. In "ready-to-hand," which is the preontological mode of human existence thrown in the world, we accept and use the things in consciousness with no conscious experience of them, i.e., without thinking about them or giving them any meaning or signification outside of their intended usage. Heidegger's example is that of using a hammer in hammering. We use a hammer without thinking about it or giving it any other condition of possibility outside of its intended usage as defined by those whose historicity presupposes our own. In "present-at-hand," which, according to Heidegger, is the stance of science, we objectify the things of consciousness and attempt to determine and reify their meanings, usage, and conditions of possibilities. Hence the hammer is intended for hammering by those who created it as a thing solely meant as such. The "unready-to-hand" outlook is assumed when something goes wrong in our usage of a thing of consciousness as defined and determined by those who adopt a "present-at-hand" view. As in the case of the hammer, the unready-to-hand view is assumed when the hammer breaks and we have to objectify it, by then assuming a present-at-hand position, and think about it in order to either reconstitute it as a hammer, or give it another condition of possibility. Any other condition of possibility that we give the hammer outside of its initial condition of possibility which presupposed our historicity becomes relational, defined in relation to any of its other conditions of possibilities it may have been given by others we exist in the world with. Hence for Heidegger, the ontological status of being-in-the-world-with-

others, via these three stances or modes of encountering the objects of consciousness hermeneutically reveal, through our view, experience, understanding, and usage of the predefined objects of knowledge, truth, and experience. Whereas Heidegger in his phenomenological work goes on to deal
with the existential themes of anxiety, alienation, death, despair, etc. in my
phenomenological stance regarding societal constitution or Beings-as-
such's-being-in-the-world-with-others via our stances to the body, language,
ideology, ideological apparatuses, communicative discourse, and social relations of production I am not concerned with the phenomenological preoccu-
pation of individual solipsistic existence as defined in Jean-Paul Sartre's
work which claims to take off from Heidegger. Instead, I am interested in the
universal ontological structure, i.e., social structure or societal constitution
and practical consciousness, which arises out of Heidegger's three stances,
what I am calling phenomenological structuralism, vis-à-vis embodiment,
language, ideology, ideological apparatuses, communicative discourse, and
social relations of production. That is, I am not concerned with Sartre's
phenomenologization of the Cartesian *res cogitans*/ transcendental ego, i.e.,
the present-at-hand transcendental ego, which he gives ontological status in
the world as a solipsistic individual seeking to define themselves for themselves lest they be declared living in bad faith. In my view, the overemphasis
of that particular aspect of *Dasein* is a product of a specific historical and
relational mode of production, and only account for one of its analytics as
highlighted by Heidegger. For me, the transcendental ego, which is a part of
a universal *élan vital*, the primeval pan-psychic field, existing in another
dimension at the subatomic particle level, does not originate out of the historical material world, but several variations of it becomes objectified via embodiment and the aforementioned stances in a universe, galaxy, and historical
material world structured by other embodied Beings and their stances. Upon
death its historicity via subatomic neuronal particles gets reabsorbed into the
élan vital, primeval pan-psychic field, to be recycled to produce future beings. As such consciousness, i.e., practical consciousness, is a product of the
stances of *Dasein* vis-à-vis its embodied recycled past consciousnesses/im-
pulses, language and ideology, which can be deferred in ego-centered communicative discourse, and structural reproduction and differentiation determined by mode of production, ideological apparatuses, and those in power
positions. Be that as it may, as with Heidegger, who refutes Sartre's existential rendering of his phenomenological ontology, I am interested in the objec-
tified/reified societal constitution and practical consciousnesses of the
transcendental egos and their relations that emerge within a dominant constitution of Being that controls a material resource framework of the world via
bodies, mode of production, language, ideology, ideological apparatuses, and
communicative discourse vis-à-vis the stances of the transcendental ego.

Hence the understanding here is that the transcendental ego of Being becomes embodied and objectified in a material resource framework enframed by bodies, the mode of production, language, ideology, ideological apparatuses, and communicative discourse of those who control a material resource framework. As embodied consciousness the transcendental ego initially encounters itself and the world in the ready-to-hand preontological mode. This means as aggregated recycled subatomic particle, Being is, initially, unconsciously driven by the drives of its body and the agential initiatives or impulses of recycled past subatomic neuronal particles as limited by their embodiment. If its drives or impulses are uninhibited by the bodies, mode of production, language, ideology, ideological apparatuses, and communicative discourse, i.e., social class language game, of those who control the material resource framework, Being may spend all of their existence in this stance. However, should they encounter resistance vis-à-vis their drives and the social class language game of those who control the material resource framework, Being moves to the unready-to-hand stance where they think about and question their own drives and or those of the material resource framework. At which point, they may become present-at-hand and may opt for either the practices associated with their internal drive or impulses, which they reify as culture, or that of the social class language game in power. If they choose the latter, being simply seeks the structural practices and differentiation of power at the expense of their internal drive. In the former case, choosing to reproduce their internal drives, impulses, or deferred meaning of linguistic structures, Being, attempts to recursively reproduce what was the unconscious drives of recycled past consciousnesses, the body, or deferred meaning in the conscious present-at-hand stance at the threat to their ontological security in the material resource framework. At which point they may seek other Beings who share their drives, impulses, deferred meaning, or seek to change the ideology of power to accept what has become a decentered subject who has deferred the meaning of power. The latter position is the basis for postmodern and post-structural thought, and alternative practices outside of structural reproduction and differentiation.

Phenomenological structuralism, therefore, seeks to highlight the ontological universal modes of embodied human existence with others, which relationally has emerged out of the phenomenological processes (Heidegger's three stances) of the transcendental ego experiencing, interpreting, and using the representational facts of its embodiment vis-à-vis the world as defined by and in the language game of others who control objects of a material resource framework, and how these modes of human existence come to (re) shape practical consciousness and constitute social structure or societal constitution. It is within this Wittgensteinian/Marxian/Heideggerian derivative ontology I explore the origins of Haitian practical consciousness as the Vodou Ethic and the spirit of communism as it stands against the Catholic/Protestant Ethic and the spirit of capitalism of the whites and Affranchis of the island.

Generally speaking, consciousnesses for me then are the embodiment of recycled subatomic neuronal energies of the multiverse objectified in the space-time of multiverses. Once objectified and embodied the neuronal energies encounter the space-time of physical worlds via a transcendental subject of consciousnesses and the sensibilities and form of the understanding of the body and brain in reified structures of signification, language, ideology, and ideological apparatuses, defined and determined by other beings that control the resources (economics) of the material world required for physical survival in space-time. The stances, ready-to-hand, unready-to-hand, and present-at-hand, of the transcendental ego vis-à-vis, 1) the sensibilities or drives of the body and brain, 2) impulses of embodied residual memories of past recycled subatomic particles, 3) the actions produced via the body in relation to the indeterminacy/deferment of meaning of linguistic and symbolic signifiers as they appear to individuated consciousnesses in ego-centered communicative discourse, 4) and the differentiating effects of the structures of signification, social class language game, of those who control the economic materials of a world is the origins of practical consciousnesses. All four types of actions, the drives or sensibilities of the body, impulses of embodied recycled past consciousnesses, structural reproduction/differentiation, and deferential actions arising via the present-at-hand stance, exist in the material world with the physical, mental, emotional, ideological, etc. powers of those who control the material resource framework via the mode of production, language, ideology, and ideological apparatuses as the causative agent for individual behaviors.

In other words, our stances in consciousness vis-à-vis the drives of the body, structural reproduction and differentiation, embodied (impulses of) past consciousnesses of recycled subatomic particles, and deferential actions resulting from the deferment of meaning in ego-centered communicative discourse determines the practical consciousness we want to recursively reorganize and reproduce in the material world. Those who control, through their bodies, language, mode of production, ideology, ideological apparatuses, and communicative discourse, the material resource framework, however, determines what actions they will allow to manifest without the embodied individual facing alienation, marginalization, or death.

As such, phenomenological structuralism synthesizes, the notions of the materialism and indeterminacy of behavior of recycled subatomic particles in quantum mechanics as they get objectified as neuronal energies of the brain and body to produce the transcendental subject of consciousness; with the potentiality for the multiplicity of choice or meaning in Heideggerian phenomenology (Heidegger's analytic of Dasein) to capture the process of indeterminacy and deferment of meaning highlighted by postmodern and post-structural theory; with Marxist dialectic and Wittgensteinian notions of language games to highlight the reified atomic structures, bodies, mode of production, language, ideology, and ideological apparatuses, collectively understood here under the concept social class language game, which attempts to structure the indeterminacy of consciousness at the atomic human level as revealed in the practices, i.e., practical consciousnesses, of social actors.

As such, the notion of *language game* utilized here is an adoption of the "language-games" later philosophy of Ludwig Wittgenstein (1953) conceptualized within a Marxian understanding of the constitution of identities based on the practical consciousness and ideology of those who control the economic conditions, social relations of production, of a material resource framework. For the Wittgenstein of the *Philosophical Investigations* language is a tool and must be thought of as a rule-governed, self-contained practice, like a game, of activities associated with some particular family of linguistic expressions, which have no point outside themselves, but is simply associated with the satisfactions they give to the participants and their form of life. What I am suggesting here, against the genetic ontology of Christopher Macann (1993) who views the transcendental ego as "a subjectification of embodied human being," in my phenomenological ontology, phenomenological structuralism, which seeks to highlight the phenomenology of being-in-the-structure-of-those-who-control-a-material-resource-framework-in-space-time through bodies, language, ideology, ideological apparatuses, and the social relations of production, i.e., *being-in-time*, is that embodiment is the objectification of the transcendental ego, which is a part of an universal *élan vital* (which is a material thing, the subatomic particles of past consciousnesses, the eternal recurrence of past consciousnesses, that gets encapsulated in the brain of breathing subjects we see in any given historical formation) that has ontological status in dimensions existing at the subatomic particle level and gets embodied as and via the connectome of Beings' brains and their bodies. Embodiment is the multiverse manifesting itself as embodied consciousness or a transcendental ego. Once objectified, materialized, and embodied as human individual consciousnesses in a present historical formation the transcendental ego becomes an embodied hermeneutic structure that never encounters the world and the things of the world in themselves as highlighted by Jacques Lacan through his conception of the symbolic. Instead embodied hermeneutic individual consciousnesses are constituted via, and as, recycled neuronal energies of past consciousnesses, the body, language, and ego-centered communicative discourse in their encounter and interpretation of things either ready-to-hand, unready-to-hand, and present-at-hand enframed in and by the historical consciousness, language, bodies, ideology, ideological apparatuses, and practices, i.e., language game, of those who control the economic conditions, social relations of production, of the material resource framework it finds itself thrown in. As embodied consciousness, whose ideas and practices are revealed and manifested through the body and language, it (individual consciousnesses of beings) can either accept (ready-to-hand) the signified historical structural knowledge, differentiation, and practices (social class language game) of those who control the economic conditions, social relations of production, of the material resource framework and recursively reorganize and reproduce them in their practices and institutions, or reject them (in the unready-to-hand and present-at-hand stance), given the ability to defer meaning in ego-centered communicative discourse, for an indeterminate amount of action-theoretic ways-of-being-in-the-world-with-others-in-space-time, which they may assume at the threat to their ontological security. It is the ready-to-hand drives of the body, ready-to-hand and present-at-hand manifestation of past recycled residual consciousnesses, the present-at-hand phenomenological meditation and deferment of meaning that occurs in embodied consciousness via language, ideology, and communicative discourse as reflected in diverse individual practices, within the ready-to-hand, unready-to-hand, and present-at-hand differentiating logic or class divisions of the social relations of production, which produces the variability of actions and practices in cultures, social structures, or social systems. All four types of actions, the drives of the body and residual past consciousnesses, structural reproduction/differentiation, and actions resulting from the deferment of meaning in ego-centered communicative discourse, are always present and manifested in a social structure (which is the reified ideology via ideological apparatuses, their social class language game, of those who control a material resource framework) to some degree contingent upon the will and desires of the economic social class that controls the material resource framework through its body, language, symbols, ideology, ideological apparatuses, and social relations of production. They choose, amidst the class division of the social relations of production, what other meaning constitutions and practices are allowed to manifest themselves without the Beings of that practice facing alienation, marginalization, domination, or death.

In sum, phenomenological structuralism posits consciousness to be the by-product or evolution of subatomic particles unfolding with increasing levels of abstraction. Subatomic particles, via the Higgs boson particle, gave rise to carbon atoms, molecules and chemistry, which gave rise to DNA, biological organisms, neurons and nervous systems, which aggregated into bodies and brains that gave rise to the preexisting consciousness of the subatomic particles, bodies, and languages. In human beings, the indeterminate behavior of subatomic neuronal energies that produced the plethora of consciousnesses and languages in the neocortex of the brain gave rise to ideologies, which in turn gave rise to ideological apparatuses and societies (sociology) under the social class language game or language, ideology, and ideological apparatuses of those who organize and control the material resources required for physical (embodied) survival in a particular resource framework. So contrary to Karl Marx's materialism which posits human consciousness to be the product of material conditions, the logic here is a structural Marxist one. That is, the aggregated, atomic, mature human being is a body and neuronal drives that never encounters the (ontological) material world directly. Instead, they encounter the (ideological) world via structures of signification, which structures the world or a particular part of it through the body, language, ideology, and ideological apparatuses, i.e., social class language game, of those whose power and power positions dictate how the resources of that framework are to be gathered, used, and distributed (means and mode of production).

PHENOMENOLOGICAL STRUCTURALISM
DIAGRAMMATICALLY

Hence phenomenological structuralism agrees with the structurationists that in the constitution of society the individual elements incorporate the structure of the ideological whole and gets differentiated by the relational logic of that whole. My understanding, unlike that of the traditional structurationists, attempts to provide an analytical tool to explain and examine the relation of the "others" within the totality who do not, however: the relationship between "the individual elements [, who,] internalize [and recursively reproduce,] the structur[ing ideology] of the whole," and those who as a result of their ready-to-hand, unready-to-hand, and present-at-hand stances vis-à-vis the drives of their bodies, residual past consciousnesses of recycled subatomic particles or through self- reflection or phenomenological meditation in the unready-to-hand and present-at-hand mode of encountering the structural terms of a society conceive of, or choose among, fully visible "alternative" ways of being-in-the-world, which they attempt to exercise in the "totality."

This "mechanical" relationship can be expressed diagrammatically (see Figure 1), and is an adaptation of Stephen Slemon's (1995) description of colonialism's multiple strategies for regulating Europe's others (Slemon, 1995, pg. 46), and the way I see it, whether in my usage of it or Slemon's slightly different depiction, it is a macro, at the societal level, extrapolation of Hegel's and Marx's master/slave dialectical power model, which would proceed along line A1, since we both suppose that our respective concepts (colonialism for Selmon and society, culture, structure, what have you, for me) are ideological or discursive formations constituted through power relations.[3]

The general understanding, within a phenomenological structural understanding of the constitution of society and practical consciousness, is that individual actors or network of solidarity or cultural groups (irreducibly "mediating" situated subjects), represented by lines "A" and "B" on the diagram, are relationally socialized within society—its semiotic field or predefined and predetermined lexicons and representations of signification (at the bottom of the diagram) i.e., the field of socialization "and its investment in reproducing and naturalising the structures of power" (Slemon, 1995, pg. 47)—through "ideological apparatuses" (at the top of the diagram) controlled by socialized institutional regulators ("As"), power elites or those in power positions, who recursively reorganize and reproduce the rules of conduct (which appear to be natural and commonsensical) of the social structure, which in modern times represent an ideological flanking for the protestant/ capitalist economic subjugation running along line "A1." Where in the first instance (A) there is encountering of the rules of conduct of the society at the preontological ready-to-hand mode of encountering, there is adoption or internalization (the Structurationist view) on behalf of the individual or network of groups of the prescribed understanding of the representations and practices of the semiotic field, i.e., the recursively organized and reproduced rules of conduct which are sanctioned. In the second (B), the individual encounters the facts and values of the world in either unready-to-hand or the present-at-hand mode, and through a form of phenomenological meditation on the structural terms (i.e., norms, values, prescriptions and proscriptions of power) that presuppose their existence, conceives of, or chooses among other or fully visible alternatives (other "Bs" discriminated by the social structure), a different understanding (, i.e., practical means, arriving from the drives of the body, unconscious drives of recycled subatomic particles, or through the deferment of meaning in ego-centered communicative discourse) of being-in-the-world ; or as in the case of racism, sexism, and classism is prescribed a structurally differentiated unalterable subordinate role based on the relational binary logic (rules for inclusion and exclusion) of the semiotic field of those in power positions ("As"). In this structurally differentiated mode the encountering is always either at the ready-to-hand or unready-to-hand mode of encountering, in the latter because something, discriminatory effects of the totality, is wrong in allowing the social actor to partake in the rules of conduct of the society. So regardless if they accept or reject the rules of conduct, they are still classified by the power elites as (Bs).

The socialized individuals or groups ("As")—socialized in the "constitutive power of societal apparatuses like the church, education, etc., and the constitutive power of fields of knowledge [, which stems from the semiotic field,] within those apparatuses" (46)—possess the potential to become, if they so choose, power elites and as such institutional regulators (at the top of the diagram), who subordinate through the manufacture of consent. Now to maintain power, those who become regulators (some "As") must address "B's" signification, which relationally undermines (it gives social actors an "alternative" form of being-in-the-world), as well as define, delimits, and stabilizes the predefined lexicons and representations of signification that is the society's semiotic field. In other words, their ("Bs'") interpretations or structurally differentiated identity in relation to "A's" reject the singularity and realism or naturalism attached to the representations and meanings of the social field, while at the same time helping to constitute it by defining, delimiting, and stabilizing the field, i.e., "B's" interpretation in relation to "A's" helps to define, because it is not, "A's" interpretation. Hence, the "As" must negotiate, appropriate, and reinflect "Bs" interpretive-practices into the semiotic field in order to delimit, their own; this is done, or has been done, up to this point in the human archaeological records on the constitution of society, by having them ("Bs") remain outside the field, by dismissing their interpretive-claims, in which case the field justifies their permanent outsider status (oppressed or discriminated against minorities, i.e., marginalized "other").

The "Bs," for the most part, can either accept (if their gaze is upon the eye of power—"As"—for recognition as a structurally differentiated "other," i.e., a class-in-itself) their appropriation, the rationale the institutional regulators ("As") prescribe to their ("B_1s'") interpretive-practical consciousness which legitimates it as a representation, or they ("B_2s") may choose (by averting their gaze as a class-for-itself) to remain *quasi*-outsiders if the meaning disclosed by the dominant institutional regulators is not in accordance with their own, or a previously discriminated subculture's, interpretive-practical understanding of the signifiers of the social structure. Regardless of what choice they ("Bs") make, however, they, "Bs," because the validity claims the institutional regulators provide for their (Bs') understanding validates their existence to start with, constantly attempt incorporation and acceptance, either, as a "class-in-itself," pushing for integration as a structurally differentiated "other" (hybrid) who recursively reproduce the rules of conduct of the social structure ("B_1s'"); or separation ("B_2s'"), as a "class-for-itself," for their own rules of conduct which are sanctioned by the power elites of the subculture. The former is the position of the bourgeoisie's of once discriminated against groups, such as blacks, women, etc., in contemporary postindustrial Protestant capitalist societies seeking to partake as an hybrid other in the social class language games of the society.

Thus there are two fundamental paths which are open to "Bs": first, if they (B) accept the understanding of (A), regarding their interpretation as an "other," and seek integration, as a structurally differentiated "class-in-itself," they have to give up their interpretive-practical consciousness, which on the one hand undermines the legitimation of the interpretive community they are classed with, while on the other hand, legitimating society's semiotic field, which has appropriated their ("Bs'") understanding and representation to substantiate and delimit their (As') power position and "practical consciousness." From this perspective, the "Bs," "B₁s'",who accept appropriation, are socialized (institutionalized) and attempt to live as ("As"), which entail recursively organizing and reproducing, as a hybrid "other," the rules of conduct of the society which are sanctioned. Those who do not (the second path), that is, those in the present-at-hand mode of encountering who reject the rules of conduct of the society, for their own, "B₂s'", may seek to reconstitute society in line with their interpretive-practical consciousness, which gives rise to another (warring) structure of signification or form of being-in-the-world, which, as a segregated categorical boundary or alternative practical consciousness, relationally and differentially delimits that of the society or social structure, which they initially constituted.[4]

From the perspective of power, "As," "Bs'" interpretations, their interpretive-practical consciousness, are always represented in the semiotic field in order to define, delimit, and stabilize the power structure. Thus, "Bs" are always oppressed minorities or majorities, i.e., "others," in the Hegelian master/slave relationship (A1), who must construct their identities or consciousness within two or more ideals: that of the social structure (master's own understanding of themselves) and what it says of the discriminated against "other" (the slave). Hence, the "Bs," as long as their gaze is turned back upon the eyes of power (vector of motion of "B₁s'") for recognition in the unready-to-hand mode of encountering, which seeks to fix the status quo for their participation, pose no real danger to the semiotic field, unless—following the aforementioned second path,"B₂s',"—they should take-up arms against it as a distinct structuring structure, i.e., "class-for-itself" or categorical boundary, which has averted their gaze, and are attempting to preserve or universalize their "alternative" ontology or "practical consciousness." This latter position is represented by Islamic fundamentalists contemporarily, and the African participants of Bois Caiman during the Haitian Revolution.

In other words, in having to construct their (Bs) identities or consciousness by warring against the ideals of the social structure, which become the relational terms that defines, delimits, and stabilizes the social structure and that by which all ("As" and "Bs") must construct their consciousness, the gaze back upon the eye of power is a sign of recognition of the validity claims of the social structure, which necessarily implies that in order to be recognized the "Bs" must attempt to be what they are not, like "As." This agential move to be like "As," however, constrains the variability of practices, which, as the diagram highlights, can only be maintained if the gaze of Bs' (vector of motion of "B₂s'") are averted away from the eyes of power in order to establish another segregated structuring structure, which celebrates and reproduces the practices' of their "otherness." So long as the aim of "B" is for acceptance into the structure of social relations that constitute the society, their "otherness" can only be expressed as those ("As") who recursively reorganize and reproduce the rules of conduct of the social structure. For it is only upon the world of existing state of affairs, i.e., the valid norms and subjective experiences of power, which is taken to be the nature of reality and existence as such, will they ("Bs") be admitted into the structure of social relations that constitute the society, for any other form may undermine the whole of social relations that is the constituted society.[5]

THE ROLE OF POWER IN THE DIAGRAM

Whereas, figure 2.1 demonstrates the action of individual social actors or groups within "a" reified consciousness, social class language game, that forms the structure of relations that is their society, figure 2.2 makes evident the actions of social actors (As), if and when, they become institutional/ideological regulators or power elites.

The understanding here is that it is the legal regulations of a society, its "lexicons and representations of signification," its rules of conduct that are sanctioned, as outlined by the power elites, or institutional regulators in power positions, which represent the objective conditions (social structure) of society that structure social relations and constitute the materials by-which

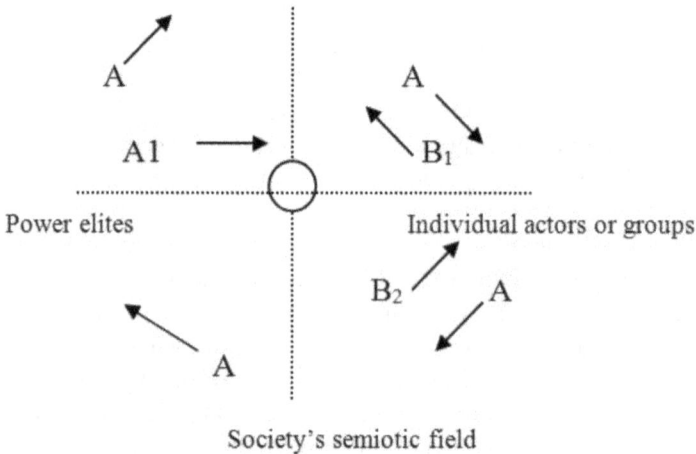

Society's semiotic field

Figure 2.1.　Institutional regulators (Society's educational/ideological apparatuses). Diagram representing the nature of the relationship between society and the individual or group in phenomenological structuralism. "A" represent the power elites of the social structure; B_1 represent those "others" (hybrids) with their gaze upon the eye of power seeking to be like "A"; B_2 represent those with their gaze averted from the eye of power seeking to exercise an alternative practical consciousness from that of "As" and "B_1s."

embodied consciousness is to be cultivated for the ontological security of the individual. In other words, the general understanding, within a phenomeno-logical structural understanding, is that individual actors or groups (irredu-cibly situated subjects), lines A and B, are socialized within society—its semiotic field or predefined and predetermined lexicons and representations of signification (at the bottom of the diagram) i.e., the field of socialization "and its investment in reproducing and naturalising the structures of power" (Slemon, 1995, pg. 47)—through "ideological apparatuses" (at the top of the diagram) controlled by socialized institutional regulators ("As"), which rep-resent an ideological flanking for the economic subjugation running along line "A1." The relation between the two runs this way: societal power oper-ates through a complex relationship between apparatuses (i.e., the law, edu-cation, rituals, family etc.) placed on line "C," where in the first instance institutional regulators ("As")—at the top of the line—appropriate and manu-facture, based on what is already understood, lexicons and representations of signification of individuals in order to consolidate and legitimate itself as a natural "order" and to reproduce individuals as deployable units of that order. So, in the first instance, societal power runs not just through the middle ground of this diagram (A1) but through a complex set of relations happen-ing along line "C;" and since the argument here is that a function (i.e., socialized social actor) at the top of this line is employing those representa-tions created at the bottom of the line in order to make up "knowledges" that have an ideological function, one can say that the vector of motion along line C is an upward one, and that this upward motion is part of the whole complex discursive structure whereby society manufactures individuals and thus helps to regulate societal relations. This is the first position.

The second position, as the diagram demonstrates, is the downward movement of societal power, where the institutional regulators of society's apparatuses are understood to be at work in the production of a purely unique and entirely projected idea of the individual, relationally delimited by other fully visible marginalized "alternative" forms of the individual being-in-the-world. The point this movement, which is inextricably tied to the first, is trying to articulate is that society is a product of the working and reworking of reified psychic projections, i.e., ideologies and their apparatuses. Hence, society has to be understood as a structure or system of power relations in which those in power positions attempt to structure, via bodies, language, ideology, ideological apparatuses, and communicative discourse individuals toward an unchangeable unified end.[6] This does not mean that there is no agency, for whom or what acts oppositionally, in this understanding of the constitution of society, is demonstrated through an understanding of the movements of lines A and B described above.

Essentially, then, in this phenomenological structural understanding, soci-ety develops from the interpretive-practical consciousness of those (power

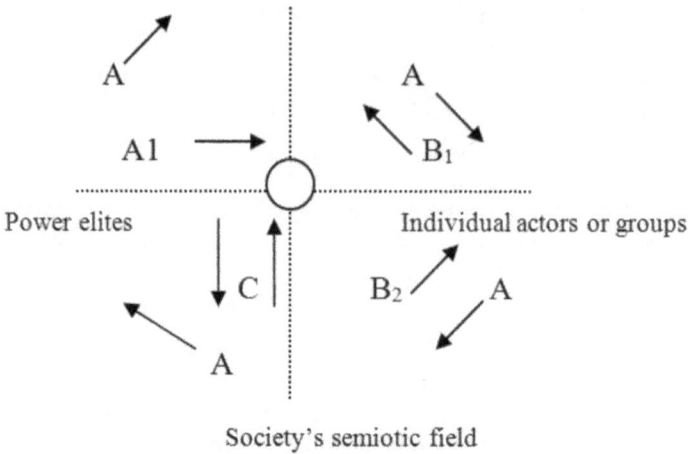

Society's semiotic field

Figure 2.2.   Institutional regulators (Society's educational/ideological apparatuses). Diagram representing the nature of the relationship—C—between society's semiotic field (bottom of diagram) and the institutional regulators (top of diagram) in phenomenological structuralism.

elites or social actors in power positions) who maintain control of and integrate its material resource framework.[7] Through this economic and political process, all individual actors ("As" and "Bs"), unless they choose (as a "class-for-itself" under the auspices of their own power elites) to establish their own institutions, are socialized in apparatuses controlled by these social actors, institutional regulators (at the top of the diagram), who employ their representations, the reified symbolic objects that constitute the semiotic field (society)—at the bottom of the diagram, in institutions—so as to control, guide, and incorporate the ambivalence that lies in the act of interpretation (Bhabha, 1995, pg. 208)—in order to make up and reproduce ideological "knowledges" that maintain the functioning of the society as a whole.[8] I am arguing that this model, up to this point in the human archaeological research on societal relations, is a general structure for understanding the multivalent strategies at work in the reproduction and transformation of societies. Furthermore, it resolves the issue of agency, which is problematic when one posits ideology or discourse or psychic processes as constructing human subjects, for who or what acts is clearly demonstrated in the model through the praxis of the structure ("As") and anti-structural elements ("Bs" if they form interpretative communities, "B_2s'", which do not seek incorporation or cooptation).

DISCUSSION AND CONCLUSIONS

Hence, the logic here is that Karl Marx's materialism is the product of the first group of embodied human beings initial encounter with the material world. Upon that initial ready-to-hand encounter, driven by the drives of the body and impulses of subatomic particles, two present-at-hand worldviews emerged and became reified via mode of production, language, ideologies, ideological apparatuses, and communicative discourse. In a fruitful and bountiful environment, as early humankind encountered ready-to-hand in Africa prior to their migration elsewhere, a harmonious disposition towards the world took hold, which was juxtaposed against an antagonistic disposition arising from a lack of resources, etc., as was found among Europeans who migrated out of Africa to Europe. According to Cheik Anta Diop (1981, 1988, 1989), as a result of these experiences African and most people of color on the earth, the Taino people of the Caribbean, for example, who inherited hospitable environments, shared certain linguistic and cultural commonalities that formed a tapestry that laid the basis, present-at-hand, for African cultural unity, which was reified and diametrically opposed to the European cultural unity that would develop, unready-to-hand and present-at-hand, in the barren and harsh environments of Europe as early humans migrated out of Africa.

What Diop called the Southern Cradle-Egyptian Model (African): 1) Abundance of vital resources, 2) Sedentary-agricultural, 3) Gentle, idealistic, peaceful nature with a spirit of justice, 4) Matriarchal family, 5) Emancipation of women in domestic life, 6) territorial state, 7) Xenophilia, 8) Cosmopolitanism, 9) Social Collectivism, 10) Material solidarity—alleviating moral or material misery, 11) Idea of peace, justice, goodness, and optimism, and 12) Literature emphasizes novel tales, fables, and comedy, emerged, present-at-hand, among the people of color in tropical climates with bountiful resources. This Southern Cradle-Egyptian Model was diametrically opposed to an unready-to-hand and present-at-hand Northern Cradle-Greek Model: (European), 1) Bareness of resources, 2) Nomadic-hunting (piracy), 3) Ferocious, warlike nature with spirit of survival, 4) Patriarchal family, 5) Debasement/enslavement of women, 6) City state (fort), 7) Xenophobia, 8) Parochialism, 9) Individualism, 10) Moral solitude, 11) Disgust for existence, pessimism, 12) Literature favors tragedy. The European/Greek model, over time became reified and recursively reorganized and reproduced, present-at-hand, as the Protestant Ethic and the spirit of capitalism under the leadership of Pastors, merchants, and owners in their encounter with Christiantiy; and the former, African model, as the Vodou Ethic and the spirit of communism under the leadership of priests, priestesses, healers, and elders (*oungan, manbo, gangan,* and *granmoun* in the Kreyol language of African/Taino/Haitian Vodou).

Hence unlike Karl Marx, which views the origins of modern capitalist relations of production via the notion of primitive accumulation, phenomenological structuralism is in agreement with Max Weber and views it as the product of the (ideological) structures of signification of European Protestant Christianity, i.e., the Protestant Ethic and the spirit of capitalism reified via ideological apparatuses based on the mode of production, which I juxtapose against the African Vodou Ethic and spirit of communism of the original inhabitants of the earth who, because of their material abundance, did not develop an antagonistic present-at-hand view of the world as their European counterparts who experienced hardship in satisfying their basic needs. In other words, African peoples, and other people of color originally inhabited the earth, ready-to-hand, in environments with abundance of vital resources. Over time, their tribal and village leaders developed present-at-hand structural ideologies, Vodou; ideological apparatuses, villages, Lakous, peristyles, *lwa yo*, and herbal medicine; and modes of productions, subsistence agriculture, husbandry, and komes that reified their experiences and formed a tapestry, i.e., social class language game under the leadership of *oungan yo, manbo yo*, and *granmoun yo* (elders) that laid the basis for African cultural/ structural unity, which was diametrically opposed to a European cultural/ structural unity that encountered, ready-to-hand, a barren material resource framework.[9]

The latter because they were unable to satisfy their bodily needs in the barren material resource framework of Europe, in other words, became unready-to-hand and developed an antagonistic stance vis-à-vis the world, which became reified, present-at-hand, as the Protestant Ethic and the spirit of capitalism when they encountered Christianity under the leadership, initially, of Pastors and merchants. Hence, what Cheikh Anta Diop called the Southern Cradle-Egyptian Model (African), which I call the Vodou Ethic and the spirit of communism social class language game, emerged, ready-to-hand and present-at-hand, among the Africans, and the Northern Cradle-Greek (European) Model, or the Protestant Ethic and the spirit of capitalism social class language game, emerged, unready-to-hand and present-at-hand, among the Europeans. The latter sought embourgeoisement and domination, and the former, ounganification/manboification, harmony, balance, perfection, and subsistence living, both models, or structuring structures, interpellated individual Beings of their material resource frameworks via different modes of production, languages, ideologies, ideological apparatuses, and communicative discourses. Both models converged on the island of Hispaniola, at the height of the slave trade and African enslavement during the eighteenth century, where the enslaved Africans of Haiti juxtaposed the latter against the former in the attempt to overthrow it on the island.

NOTES

1. Within my phenomenological structural sociology, the concepts of postmodern, post-structural, and postcolonial theories represent the practical consciousness of the "other" bourgeoisies.

2. My phenomenological structuralism, as in Western epistemology and ontology which developed as a result of the ever-increasing rationalization and testing of Christian notions, reflects my rationalization of Vodou metaphysics as an ontology and sociology for understanding cosmic and societal constitution. As such, my work builds off of Reginald O. Crosley's (2006) essay, "Shadow-Matter Universes in Haitian and Dagara Ontologies: A Comparative Study," whose physics I summarize here.

3. For an in-depth look at Slemon's diagram and description see: Slemon, Stephen (994). "The Scramble for Post-colonialism." In *De-Scribing Empire: Post-colonialism and Textuality*, Eds. Chris Tiffin and Alan Lawson. London: Routledge. Slemon borrows this model (see figure 1 in the text) from De Saussure (1983 [1916]: 80), who prescribes the model as means for all sciences to map out the things they are concerned with. He calls the horizontal axis, "the axis of simultaneity." "This axis concerns relations between things which coexist, relations from which the passage of time is entirely excluded." The vertical axis, "the axis of succession:" "Along this axis one may consider only one thing at a time. But here we find all the things situated along the first axis, together with the changes they undergo."

Slemon, in using this model to understand Edward Said's depiction of colonialism and the role of the "other" argues, as many critics of structuralism have done, that there is no agency regardless of the practices taking place along the diachronic axis (i.e., the vertical axis; the horizontal axis for Saussure is the synchronic). Using this model to depict what I mean by phenomenological structuralism, I am arguing that my description is not historically specific, and resolves the issue of agency in structure (in this case ideological structure or hegemony).

4. Some may point to a third alternative, i.e., subversion from within, but this is a misconception because in order to be a subverter, the social actor must still recursively reorganize and reproduce the practical consciousness of the whole.

5. In other words, although "Bs" in the diagram represent the variability of praxis within structure, "counter-movements" in the Polanyian (2001 [1944]) sense only refer to embodied variable practices—which diametrically oppose the structuring end of the society or social structure they constitute and delimit—which seek to reconstitute society. As long as the aim of the discriminated against minority ("Bs") is for recognition as an "other," the variability of praxis is negated by the non-subversive hybridity of the discriminated against social actor.

6. According to the Structuralism of De Saussure, "[c]hange originates in linguistic performance, in *parole* [(i.e., speech, practice, or event)], not in *la langue* [(formal structure or institutions)], and what is modified are individual elements of the system of realization. Historical changes affect the system in the end, in that the system will adjust to them, make use of the results of historical change, but it is not the linguistic system which produces them" (Culler, 1976, pg. 41). From a phenomenological structural perspective what this means is that the ends to which the structure of society is directed appears to be unchangeable, even though the interpretive-practices amongst individuals and groups are, and may even contradict that appearance. What happens in the end is that institutional regulators attempt to incorporate these differential interpretive-practices in a way to maintain the order of things so that the end to which society is structured continues to be realizable in spite of the differential practices. In fact, these practices, defined by their relation with the practices of the structure come to delimit the actual structure.

7. This, as André C. Drainville (1995) observes, "is the essence of what Nicos Poulantzas called the political task of transformation" (57).

8. Whereas at issue for Bourdieu, Sahlins, and Giddens "is the being of *structure* in history and as history" (Sahlins, 1985, pg. 145), my approach does not see structure and history as antinomies, and therefore, focuses on the issue of "being" in *a structure of history*, or the predefined and predetermined "lexicons and representations of signification" that attempt to reproduce an aspect of "Being." Transformation in this understanding is in the development of the historical structure as played-out in the interpretive-practices of the "Beings" or subjects of

the system. In other words, reproduction is only attempted in the actual use of the structural ideas in "ideological apparatuses." But this is only an attempt, for the ideas, as objectified by those in power, are distorted as a result of the interpretive-practices of irreducibly situated individuals. So what we have is a dynamic structure driven by interpretive-practices within what is already understood of the objectified concepts of those in power positions, who must attempt to appropriate and redirect interpretative-practices that oppose or threaten their symbolic order. In doing so the structure may or may not be transformed, for transformation rests *only* in the ability of those with contradictory understandings of the symbolic order (Bs in the diagrams) to reconstitute society based on their understanding. As long as, power (As) is able to appropriate and reinflect their (Bs) understanding, reproduction, and as such structural domination along the same structural line (horizontal axis), is the only necessary outcome.

9. I am using the Haitian/African Kreyol language for priests (oungan), priestesses (manbo), gangan (healers) and elders (granmoun), here out of convenience.

Chapter Three

A Phenomenological Structural Constitution of Modern Society

"The Protestant Ethic and the Spirit of Capitalism"

So contrary to Karl Marx's early materialism which posits human conscious-ness to be the product of material conditions, the logic here is a later structu-ral Marxist one synthesized with a Weberian sociology, which posits that the aggregated mature human being is an aggregation of "conscious" subatomic particles that never encounters the material world directly. Instead, they en-counter the world via structures of signification, which structures the world or a particular part of it through the body, consciousness, language, ideology, ideological apparatuses, and mode of production, i.e., social class language game, of those whose power and power positions dictate how the resources of that framework are to be gathered, used, and distributed (means and mode of production). Hence unlike Marx, which views the origins of modern capi-talist relations of production via the notion of primitive accumulation, my phenomenological structural ontology is in agreement with Max Weber and views it as the product of the structures of signification of Protestant Chris-tianity, i.e., the Protestant Ethic and the spirit of capitalism social class lan-guage game under the leadership of white, Protestant, pastors, merchants, and owners, which I juxtapose against the African Vodou Ethic and spirit of communism social class language game of the original inhabitants of the earth under the leadership of priests, priestesses, healers, and elders, who, because of their material abundance, did not develop an antagonistic un-ready-to-hand and present-at-hand view of the world as their European counterparts. Instead, they developed a present-at-hand worldview based on their initial ready-to-hand encountering of a material world, which readily provided them everything they needed for their existence.

In other words, African peoples, and other people of color originally inhabited the earth, ready-to-hand, in environments with abundance of vital resources. Over time, they developed present-at-hand structural ideologies and ideological apparatuses, agricultural production/*komes*, Vodou, villages, Lakous, peristyles, under the leadership of priests, priestesses, healers, and elders that formed a tapestry that laid the basis for African cultural/structural unity, which sought to keep the balance, harmony, perfection, and subsistence living they encountered within their material resource framework.

This African cultural/structural unity was diametrically opposed to a European cultural/structural unity that encountered ready-to-hand and unready-to-hand a barren material resource framework. Upon their initial ready-to-hand stance, the European was unable to satisfy their bodily needs in a barren and hostile environment. As a result, they became unready-to-hand, because their environment did not fulfill their basic needs, and sought to fulfill their basic needs through the objectification and externalization of the world, which they sought to exploit and dominate in order to meet their (bodily) needs. They reified their experiences, present-at-hand, as the nature of reality as such, which they sought to extrapolate throughout the world.

What Cheikh Anta Diop called the Southern Cradle-Egyptian Model (African), which I call the Vodou Ethic and the spirit of communism social class language game, emerged among the Africans, and the Northern Cradle-Greek (European) Model, or the Protestant Ethic and the spirit of capitalism social class language game, emerged among the Europeans when they encountered Christianity. The former is characterized as and based on, 1) Abundance of vital resources, 2) Sedentary-agricultural, 3) Gentle, idealistic, peaceful nature with a spirit of justice, 4) Matriarchal family, 5) Emancipation of women in domestic life, 6) territorial state, 7) Xenophilia, 8). Cosmopolitanism, 9) Social Collectivism, 10) Material solidarity—alleviating moral or material misery, 11) Idea of peace, justice, goodness, and optimism, and 12) Literature emphasizes novel tales, fables, and comedy. The latter is characterized as and based on, 1) Bareness of resources, 2) Nomadic-hunting (piracy), 3) Ferocious, warlike nature with spirit of survival, 4) Patriarchal family, 5) Debasement/enslavement of women, 6) City state (fort), 7) Xenophobia, 8) Parochialism, 9) Individualism, 10) Moral solitude, 11) Disgust for existence, pessimism, 12) Literature favors tragedy. Historically, the latter, European model, became constituted and reified present-at-hand as the Protestant Ethic and the spirit of capitalism under the leadership of pastors, owners, and merchants; and the former, African model, as the Vodou Ethic and the spirit of communism under the leadership of priests, priestesses, healers, and elders, i.e., oungan yo, manbo yo, gangan yo, granmoun yo.[1] Both models converged on the island of Hispaniola, at the height of the slave trade and African enslavement during the eighteenth century, where the enslaved Africans and Taino people of Haiti juxtaposed the latter against the former to overthrow it on the island.

Hence, the argument here is that the constitution of modernity is the by-product of the structuralizing and differentiating effects of the Protestant ethic and the spirit of capitalism, via agricultural, industrial, and postindustrial modes of production, European languages, Protestant ideology, and ideological apparatuses, churches, schools, etc., initially, by the practical consciousness or social class language game of religious, rich, white, Protestant, heterosexual, bourgeois, men in their rejection of the class division and social relations of production of the Catholic feudal order beginning in the sixteenth century.

Building on the rationalization of the primeval pan-psychic field within the God and soul concepts of early Christian dogma, the God of Judaism "was active in history and in current political events rather than in the primordial sacred time of myth" (Armstrong, 1993, pg. 211). Be that as it may, the traditions of Christianity and Islam inherited this sociohistorical metaphysical understanding of God, which made their central motif a confrontation or a personal meeting between God and humanity devoted to ensuring that God's will is done on earth as it is in heaven:

> This God is experienced as an imperative to action; he calls us to himself; gives us the choice of rejecting or accepting his love and concern. This God relates to human beings by means of a dialogue rather than silent contemplation. He utters a Word, which becomes the chief focus of devotion and which has to be painfully incarnated in the flawed and tragic conditions of earthly life. In Christianity, the most personalized of the three, the relationship with God is characterized by love. But the point of love is that the ego has, in some sense, to be annihilated (Armstrong, 1993, pg. 210-211).

The barbarian tribes from Europe that eventually brought down the Holy Roman Empire in the fifth century of the common era transmogrified the orientalism and aforementioned historical understanding of Christianity highlighted by Karen Armstrong to fit with their initial calculating, crude, and barbarous existence, which would subsequently become embodied, once they converted to Christianity, in the discourse and discursive practices of the Protestant Ethic and the spirit of capitalism social class language game.

The fall of the Holy Roman Empire would coincide with the rise of imperial Christianity, which began with the evangelism and feudalism of the Roman Catholic Church. The Catholic Church, following Constantine's usurpation of Christianity from the margins of the Roman Empire the fourth century of the Common Era, sought to imperially convert the world's social actors, and constitute the city of God on earth via, the family, church, feudalism and the aristocratic demeanor. Following the Protestant Reformation of the fifteenth and sixteenth centuries, they would subsequently be displaced by the imperial Christianity of the American nation-state embodied in its discourse and discursive practice, the Protestant Ethic and the spirit of capitalism, by the heteronormativity or social class language game of rich, white, Protestant, heterosexual male merchants.

Beginning in the sixteenth century of the common era, God's will on earth was no longer constituted around the ideological apparatuses of the family, church, aristocracy, and feudalism of the Catholic Church, but became interpreted as a Hobbesian imperative material struggle of" all against all" in the "flawed and tragic conditions of earthly life" wherein the most pious and egoless souls, which God calls to himself, who accept him, obtained material wealth as a sign of their personal salvation and God's grace and mercy. Protestant reformers such as the Puritans and Pilgrims zealously sought to convert all of Europe and the known world to their Protestant interpretation of the gospel of Jesus via the social class language game of the patriarchal family, Protestant churches, the modern state, class division, and social relations of mercantile and agricultural capitalist production. Their inability to constitute the city of God or their social class language game in Europe, based on their Protestantism, led to their persecution and the eventual founding of the American nation-state as the city of God grounded in the imperial Christianity of the Protestant Ethic and spirit of capitalism social class language game. This Protestant Ethic and the spirit of capitalism, which would zealously and imperially seek to displace the evangelism and feudal discourse and discursive practice of the Catholic Church, the Amerindian world worldviews, Islam, African tribalism, etc., via the patriarchal family, Protestant churches, education, the state, and capitalist relations of production, has nothing to do with the egalitarianism, compassion, and social altruistic message of Jesus as highlighted in the synoptic gospels and the gospel of John as interpreted by the Catholic church, however. Quite the reverse, it fosters class division, inequality, selfishness, self-interested individualism, and materialism reified initially in the discourse and discursive practices, social class language game, of a patriarchal, heterosexual, white male Protestantism and the spirit of capitalism, which discriminated against and marginalized all other practical consciousnesses or ways of organizing society and the world via the patriarchal family, protestant discourse of churches, schools, prisons, class division, the modern state, and the social relations of mercantile, agricultural, industrial, and post-industrial capitalist productions.

Hence with the rise to power of Western European tribes and their Protestant interpretations of Christianity over feudal aristocratic Catholic dogma, the class division and social relations of production of the Protestant ethic and the spirit of capitalism and not the egalitarian, compassionate, and social altruistic message of Jesus, as Max Weber (1958) points out, represents what was understood, the set of values—rationality, hard work, economic gain as a sign of one's predestination, systematic use of time, and a strict asceticism with respect to worldly pleasures and goods—which he claims gave rise to the contemporary capitalist practices that constitute modern societies, and thus American capitalist society, and the existing configuration of bureaucratic power relations, social class language game, within which modern social identity and practical consciousness developed.

The purposive-rationality of these Protestant ideas and practices, mediated and overdetermined by the concepts of class, race, and nation, in other words, historicized social positions, based on racial, national identity, and economic gain for its own sake (class) through the accumulation of capital or profit in a "calling," initially mercantile, agricultural, and industrial relations of production, by which social actors or subjects were differentiated and subjugated (predestined or capitalists/damned or laborers) in the society and the world. Rich, white, heterosexual men universalized, present-at-hand, their ideology, through ideological apparatuses, the patriarchal family, church, schools, prisons, the modern state, class division, and the social relations of production, against all other practical consciousnesses, African polygamous tribalism, homosexuality, etc., arrived at through drives of the body, impulses of subatomic particles, and the deferment of meaning in ego-centered communicative discourse, for their embourgeoisement. From the late seventeenth century to the present, the ideology and ideological apparatuses of the modern state, family, church, and education, class division, and the social relations of production enframed by the Protestant ethic and spirit of capitalism of rich, white, heterosexual, Protestant, men would be the structure, language, ideology, ideological apparatuses, and communicative discourse within which social identities were constituted, differentiated, discriminated against, and marginalized.

This theoretical framework differs from both Marxist and non-Marxist structural interpretations of the constitution of modern society in that it begins with the socioreligious cultural (ideal) conceptions that initially structured the social integrative practices that gave rise to the society, while the Marxist and neo-Marxist schools derive the terms from which they begin their analysis from the (material) social relations of production. These two viewpoints, systems and social integration, as my structural approach implies, are inextricably linked, however, and represents the relational structural-cultural framework organized around social relations of production, class division, and the modern state and its ideology and ideological apparatuses, i.e., nuclear family, education, prisons, etc., which determined social identity and practices in modern societies. In other words, although philosophically we are able to think these two approaches apart as idealism and materialism, they are not necessarily entirely separable in reality in my phenomenological structural logic.

Weber defines a capitalistic economic action,

as one which rests on the expectation of profit by the utilization of opportunities for exchange, that is on (formally) peaceful chances of profit. Acquisition by force (formally and actually) follows its own particular laws, and it is not expedient, however little one can forbid this, to place it in the same category with action which is, in the last analysis, oriented to profits from exchange. Where capitalist acquisition is rationally pursued, the corresponding action is adjusted to calculations in terms of capital. This means that the action is adapted to a systematic utilization of goods or personal services as means of acquisition in such a way that, at the close of a business period, the balance of the enterprise in money assets (or, in the case of a continuous enterprise, the periodically estimated money value of assets) exceeds the capital, i.e. [,] the estimated value of the material means of production used for acquisition in exchange (Weber, 1958, pg. 17-18).

Although this relationship appears paradoxical, since protestant beliefs did not embrace the idea of economic gain for its own sake,

Weber's argument is that the rational pursuit of the ultimate values of the ascetic Protestantism characteristic of sixteenth-and seventeenth-century Europe led people to engage in disciplined work; and that disciplined and rational organization of work as a duty is the characteristic feature of modern capitalism—its unique ethos or spirit (Marshall, 1998, pg. 534).

Thus,

The crucial link to Protestantism comes through the latter's notion of the calling of the faithful to fulfil their duty to God in the methodical conduct of their everyday lives. This theme is common to the beliefs of the Calvinist and neoCalvinist churches of the Reformation. Predestination is also an important belief, but since humans cannot know who is saved (elect) and who is damned, this creates a deep inner loneliness in the believer. In order therefore to create assurance of salvation, which is itself a sure sign (or proof) of election, diligence in one's calling (hard work, systematic use of time, and a strict asceticism with respect to worldly pleasures and goods) is highly recommended—so-called 'this-worldly asceticism'. In general terms, however, the most important contribution of Protestantism to capitalism was the spirit of rationalization that it encouraged. The relationship between the two is deemed by Weber to be one of elective affinity (Marshall, 1998, pg. 535).

The affinity between the Protestantism of a sect and their purposive-rational actions, as I understand Weber to be saying, gave rise to the *economic* organization of modern society, systems integration, as the social psychological practices and ego-ideals (rationally calculating individuals attempting to prove their predestination reflected in their economic gains) of a form of Protestantism, social integration, were rationally and purposively incorporated into the physical world through the bureaucratic organization of the material resource framework around language, ideology, ideological apparatuses, the patriarchal family, church, schools, state, prisons, and economy, social relations of production, in order to direct and constitute the identity and practices of social actors and societies for economic gain. (In some instances, as in the attempt of the Puritans to usurp power and takeover the English nation-state of the seventeenth century under Oliver Cromwell, bureaucratic means or structural practices—purposive-formal-rational action to organize the lived world—were established around already existing material elements which were re-conceptualized by the sect of rich, white, Protestant, men to foster a society based on wealth, economic gain or capital accumulation as a sign of their salvation in the eyes of God and others).

Thus, the sociohistorical logic here is that following the Protestant Reformations of the fifteenth and sixteenth centuries, as rich, white, heterosexual Protestant men and their ethos encountered social problems in their attempt to reconfigure or reconstitute sixteenth and seventeenth century European catholic feudal governments, mode of production, ideology, and ideological apparatuses, along the lines of their social class language game, Protestantism and social relations of production, they became a discriminated against "other" (Puritans, Pilgrims, Calvinists, Lutherans, etc.) minority in the Feudal (catholic) social structure of Europe of the middle ages. Subsequently, these newly created and marginalized "others" left Europe and reformulated society, in the form of the American social structure by recursively reorganizing and reproducing their "other" Protestant form of being-in-the-world, i.e. Protestantism and the spirit of capitalism, via the organization of the state and its ideological apparatuses, family, church, and schools, class division, and social relations of production, i.e., mercantile, agricultural, industrial, and subsequently postindustrial beginning in the 1970s.

The rules of conduct and ideological apparatuses of the new American society, in other words, were formulated to facilitate the relational logic, ends (substantive rationality), of their, rich, white, heterosexual Protestant men, form of Protestantism, individualism, humanitarianism, rationalism, economic gain, or loss, as a sign of one's election or "damned-ness" in a particular "calling," mercantile, agricultural, industrial, and postindustrial capital, which "embedded" social or cultural relations in what became the modern American political-economic system. With this sociohistorical conversion, within the Westphalian nation-state system, of Western society in general and American society in particular, from a catholic feudal social order to a Protestant capitalist social order through the purposive-rationality or social class language game of rich, white, heterosexual Protestant men against all other forms of being-in-the-world, the Protestant ethic became an allowed religion of the society, and thus the "metaphysical" ideas of the Protestant Church became joined with the power and discursive practices of the American Protestant nation-state government as organized around ideological apparatuses, i.e., prisons, the family, church, school, state, class division, and work or the social relations of production. This "invisible" marriage of church and state led to the formation of the "visible" universal ideals/ideologies (liberalism, democracy, individualism, bourgeois classism, and nationalism) of the American nation-state under god to direct the material economic practices of all social actors, and over time caused the American nation-state/ government to refine its doctrine and develop its structure in a way that best served its purposive-rational end, economic gain as a sign of the country and its citizens' salvation and predestination in mercantile, agricultural, industrial, and postindustrial social relations of production, within the emerging global (colonial) economic world-system, which they would gain control of following World War II through transnational ideological apparatuses such as the World Bank (WB), International Monetary Fund (IMF), United Nations (UN), etc.

In materialist terms, the endless accumulation of economic gain, capital, or profit by rich white heterosexual Protestant men became "the defining characteristic and *raison d' être* of this [social] system," which over time pushed "towards the commodification of everything, the absolute increase of world production, and a complex and sophisticated social division of labor based on class" or the amount of capital (economic gain) one had accumulated (Balibar and Wallerstein, 1991, pg. 107). As Jürgen Habermas concludes of this process by which the integrative substantive-rationality of a form of Protestantism, "the spirit of capitalism," came to dominate modern times by the systemic purposive-rational action of its power agents:

> . . . economic production is organized in a capitalist manner, with rationally calculating entrepreneurs [(the predestined prosper)]; public administration is organized in a bureaucratic manner, with juristically trained, specialized officials—that is, they are organized in the form of private enterprises and public bureaucracies. The relevant means for carrying out their tasks are concentrated in the hands of owners and leaders; membership in these organizations is made independent of ascriptive properties [(today, maybe, but not the case for this type of society's early formation)]. By these means, organizations gain a high degree of internal flexibility and external autonomy. In virtue of their efficiency, the organizational forms of the capitalist economy and the modern state administration establish themselves in other action systems to such an extent that modern societies fit the picture of "a society of organizations," even from the standpoint of lay members (Habermas, 1987 [1981], pg. 306).

In this understanding of the origins and organizational basis of modernity and its paragon modern American capitalist society, where "the cultural struggle for distinction is intricately connected to the economic distribution of material goods, which it both legitimates and reproduces" (Gartman, 2002, pg. 257), Weber's explanation, as Jürgen Habermas points out,

... refers in the first instance not to the establishment of the labor markets that turned abstract labor power into an expense in business calculations, but to the "spirit of capitalism," that is, to the mentality characteristic of the purposive-rational economic action of the early capitalist entrepreneurs. Whereas Marx took the mode of production to be the phenomenon in need of explanation, and investigated capital accumulation as the new mechanism of system integration, Weber's view of the problem turns the investigation in another direction. For him the explanans is the conversion of the economy and state administration over to purposive-rational action orientations; the changes fall in the domain of forms of social integration. At the same time, this new form of social integration made it possible to institutionalize the money mechanism, and thereby new mechanisms of system integration (Habermas, 1987 [1981], pg. 313).

These two analytic levels, systems and social integration, are not separate if the understanding of the constitution of modernity is understood through my phenomenological structural and organizational logic. The argument from this Althusserian structural position is that the "predestined" white Protestant entrepreneurial males, a once marginalized group in pre-modern or feudal (catholic) Europe, by re-conceptualizing and maintaining the control of the then feudal market and state within the mythical realities or social class language game of their heterosexual bourgeois male Protestantism, reified their Protestant "practical consciousness" with the state and its ideological apparatuses, prisons, family, church, schools, etc. This Protestant metaphysical cultural value or ideology, in other words, they rationalized with reality and existence as such, in institutions or ideological apparatuses, prisons, the family, church, schools, capitalist global market economy and bourgeois state, operating "through materialized metaphors beyond logical or empirical proof, on ungroundable premises, on nonobservable substances" (Friedland, 2002, pg. 384), in order to mechanically and systemically interpellate, constitute, and direct (embourgeois) the identity and agential moments or purposive-rationality of all social actors of the world for the sole purpose of accumulating economic gain (Marx's "capital accumulation") as a sign of their election or progress in the world against those who either were damned as revealed by their poverty in the social relations of production of the society, or conceived of other practical consciousnesses arrived at through the deferment of meaning in ego-centered communicative action.

Class division and the organization of work, mercantile, agricultural, industrial, and postindustrial, for economic gain or profit in modern society was mechanically constituted as white Protestant heterosexual males believing themselves to be "predestined" came as a social class to militarily dominate and control the ontological security of the world and its people of color, who, within their social class language game, they interpellated as the irrational damned or laborers working in the aforementioned social relations of

production, through subsequently global institutions or ideological apparatuses like the Protestant churches, schools, the IMF, World Bank, United
Nations, etc., in order to (re) produce economic gain for those (predestined)
who owned the means and modes of work or production. To put the matter
simply, the logic here is that "the spirit of capitalism," which is characteristic
of modernity in general and American society in particular, is the socioreligious discursive practice or purposive rationality (mythopraxis) of a form of
cultural Protestantism that gave rise to the class identity of social actors, who
became differentiated by class, race, and sexual divisions and their social
behavioral (methodical) relation to the means and mode of work in modern
societies.

The metaphysics of the Protestant Ethic as initially interpreted by rich,
white, Protestant men, in other words, structured, through their bodies, languages, ideologies (Protestantism, liberalism, racism, etc.), and ideological
apparatuses, the physical material world wherein individual social relations
and actions were constituted and (re) produced through the organization of
work, the modern state, class division, and the praxis of capitalist relations of
production.

Thus, the Enlightenment project or attempt to constitute society based on
democratically arrived at rational rules of conduct which are sanctioned
which began in the seventeenth century with philosophers and artists never
materialized as rich, white, heterosexual, bourgeois Protestant males, the
emerging power elites of the seventeenth century, incorporated the products
of scientific reason and rationality itself into their Protestant metaphysics or
social class language game so as to facilitate their purposive socioreligious
rationale of economic gain via capitalist relations of production. So it is not
that modernity and the organization of the contemporary social world under
the hegemony of the American nation-state represents the ever-increasing
rationalization of the world, which dates from the Enlightenment. Instead, it
represents the ever-increasing mystification of the world around the discursive practices, "mythopraxis" (Marshall Sahlins' term), or social class language game of the Protestant Ethic and the spirit of capitalism. The reason
and rationality of the scientific method, which comes out of the Enlightenment project, was not constituted as a distinct social class language game to
direct society under the leadership of scientists and philosophers; instead, the
rational-empiricism that would come to dominate the seventeenth century
became a facilitator for promoting the ethos of an emerging Protestantism
and the spirit of capitalism reified in the discourse and discursive practices of
the nation-state and its ideological apparatuses, i.e., education, church, family, etc., and organization of work or social relations of production under the
leadership and social class language games of rich, white, Protestant, heterosexual men.

Hence, the Americentric dominated form of modernity, neoliberalism with its emphasis on family life, individualism, education, class division, free markets, free trade, political and economic liberalism, outsourcing of jobs, privatization, etc., which contemporarily dominates the world in and through the discourse of globalization represents the continual attempt to homogenize and universalize social identities and social practices the world over to fit within the metaphysical discourse and discursive practices of agents of the Protestant Ethic who purposively rationalized the discourse of their metaphysic into the laws and practices of their society and global institutions against the metaphysics of adherents of the Enlightenment, the poor, and other metaphysics. Hence, the mythical realities of rich, white, Protestant, heterosexual bourgeois males canonized in laws and social institutions determined their praxis, and relationally attempted to determine the praxis of all "others" they encountered in their quest to prove their predestination. It should also be mentioned that modern societies in the global economic world-system, as all became interpellated as owners and workers, itself became a dialectical totality that underwent reproduction and transformation based on internal contradictions and class differentiation based upon capital accumulation motivated by the desire to acquire capital or economic gain for its own sake as prescribed by the substantive-rationality or social class language game of the Protestant Ethic and the spirit of capitalism (Balibar and Wallerstein, 1991; Smith, 1996). In fact, the modern political and economic ideologies of liberalism, conservatism, and radicalism are grounded in, and can be deduced from, the metaphysics of "the Protestant Ethic and the spirit of capitalism": radicalism representing a revolutionary response against the ideals and practices of liberal bourgeois heterosexual white male Protestantism that included bourgeois technical rationality, individualism, class inequality, racialism, and heterosexism; conservatism, representing strict commitment to its ideologies of individualism, class inequality, heterosexism, religiosity, and racialism; and liberalism was deduced from the Christian (Protestant) ethic of individual humanism, rationalism, anti-dogmatism, classism, and the liberal democratic capitalist state's ability to foster that ethic.

GLOBALIZATION

From the sixteenth century to the present, the Protestant Ethic and the spirit of capitalism social class language game under the leadership of rich, white, Protestant, heterosexual men became the structural framework within which all peoples of the world were interpellated, embourgeoised, and differentiated via European languages, white male/female bodies, ideology, ideological apparatuses of the nation-state, and modes of production. The contemporary phenomenon of globalization under American hegemony is the continuing attempt, under the leadership of an embourgeoised hybrid, multiracial, multi-sexual, multinational, etc., upper-class of owners and high-level executives, who, unready-to-hand (because of the discriminatory effects of their societies, which prevented them from participating in it), in the 1960s dialectically sought equality of opportunity, recognition, and distribution with their white counterparts, to structure the world within the structural metaphysics or social class language game of the Protestant Ethic and the spirit of capitalism against other practices and organizations of realities arrived at through the drives of the body, impulses of subatomic particles, and the deferment in ego-centered communicative discourse. Albeit the Protestant Ethic and the spirit of capitalism social class language game under American hegemony today, unlike when Weber was writing when the emphasis in the agricultural and industrial modes of producing that wealth was simply capital accumulation, is defined by economic gain for its own sake and material (personal) wealth as a sign of God's grace and blessings.[2]

Contemporarily, "culture of globalization" and the "globalization as culture" metaphors represent two sociological approaches to understanding the contemporary post-modern phenomenon we call globalization, the current configuration of the Protestant Ethic and the spirit of capitalism, under American hegemony (1970s-2000s). These two sociopolitical understandings regarding the origins and nature of globalization, as Kevin Archer et al (2007) points out, have "set off a vigorous and at times rancorous debate within the social sciences" (2007, pg. 2). On one side of the debate you have theorists who emphasize the "culture of globalization" and argue the idea that "the constitutive role of culture is critical for grasping the continued hegemony of capitalism in the form of globalization. . . Culture, they assert is increasingly being co-opted and deployed as a new accumulation strategy to broaden and deepen the frontiers of capitalism and to displace its inherent crisis tendencies" (Archer, 2007, pg. 2-3). In a word, in the continual hegemonic quest of capitalism to equalize the conditions of the world to serve capital, globalization, in the eyes of "culture of globalization" theorists, represents a stage of capitalism's development highlighted by the commodification of culture as a means for accumulating profits from the purchasing and consuming power of a transnational class of administrative bourgeoisies and professional cosmopolitan elites in core, semi-periphery, and periphery nation-states who subscribe to the social integrative norms of liberal bourgeois Protestantism (hard work, economic gain, political and economic liberalism, consumption, etc.).

In other words, the material and symbolic cultural elements of the cultures of the world are commodified by the upper class of owners and high-level executives of core countries—where finance capital and service jobs predominate—to make a profit or produce surplus-value—given the declining significance of profit from industrial production that have been shipped or outsourced to semi-periphery and periphery nations giving rise to their national bourgeoisies whose cultural practices and tastes have been national-ized—by fulfilling the consumption tastes of the financiers, administrative bourgeoisies, professional classes, and cosmopolitan elites of nation-states throughout the world who control their masses as a surplus labor force and cultural producers for global capital. Globalization, therefore, is the integra-tion of the cultural realm and individual experiences into the commodity chains of the capitalist elites, who homogenize, through the media and other "ideological state apparatuses," the behavior and tastes of global social actors as consumers thereby homogenizing the cultural practices and tastes of the middle and under class peoples of the world in order to generate profit in postindustrial economies such as the US and UK.

This "culture-of-globalization" understanding of globalization or the postmodern condition in late capitalist development is a well-supported posi-tion, which highlights, in the twenty-first century, the continued hegemony of capitalism or capitalist relations of production in the form of globalization (Hardt and Negri, 2000; Kellner, 1988; Giddens, 1991; Harvey, 1989, 1990; Jameson, 1984, 1991). This line of thinking, in which theorists point to the underlining drive of globalization as the continuing historical push to social-ly, economically, and politically (under) develop the rest of the world along the lines, or as a simulacrum, of Western American and European Societies to facilitate capital accumulation, began with European colonialism, contin-ued through the "development project" of the Cold-war era, and now is embodied in the globalization process. This historical process is highlighted in modernization, development, dependent development, world-systems the-ories, and contemporarily it is a trend outlined in the theoretical works of postmodern theorists such as David Harvey (1989, 1990) and Fredric Jame-son (1984, 1991) who view globalization as postmodern or the cultural logic of capitalist development in core or developed countries. "Culture of global-ization" theorists, such as Harvey and Jameson, therefore, view globalization as the new initiative, with the same intentions, replacing the accumulation and modernization project of colonialism and development.

The homogenization, accumulation, and "modernization" project in Euro-pean colonialism operated through the establishment of either colonies of settlement, "which often eliminate[d] indigenous people," or rule, where colonial administrators reorganize[d] existing cultures by imposing new in-equalities [(around class, gender, race, and caste)] to facilitate their exploita-tion, wherein an unequal division of agricultural (monoculture) labor was physically and psychologically forced upon the peoples of color the world over to sustain the industrial and manufacturing cultural life of Europeans, while simultaneously disrupting, destroying, and reconfiguring the cultural practices and tastes of the colonized peoples within the binary (structural) logic of the (European) colonizer (McMichael, 2008 pg. 27). As Philip McMichael (2008, pg. 31) observed of the European colonization process,

> From the sixteenth century, European colonists and traders traveled along African coasts to the New World and across the Indian Ocean and the China seas seeking fur, precious metals, slave labor, spices, tobacco, cacao, potatoes, sugar, and cotton. The principal European colonial powers—Spain, Portugal, Holland, France, and Britain—and their merchant companies exchanged manufactured goods such as cloth, guns, and implements for these products and for Africans taken into slavery and transported to the Americas. In the process, they reorganized the world.
>
> The basic pattern was to establish in the colonies specialized extraction and production of raw materials and primary products that were unavailable in Europe. In turn, these products fueled European manufacturing as industrial inputs and foodstuffs for its industrial labor force. On a world scale, this specialization between European economies and their colonies came to be termed the colonial division of labor.
>
> While the colonial division of labor stimulated European industrialization, it forced non-Europeans into primary commodity production. Specialization at each end of the exchange set in motion a transformation of social and environmental relationships, fueled by a dynamic relocation of resources and energy from colony to metropolis: an unequal ecological exchange. Not only were the colonies converted into exporters of raw materials and foodstuffs, but also they became "exporters of sustainability."

The sociocultural outcome of this exploitative and oppressive socioeconomic military system was a racialized social structural relationship relationally constituted based on the "unequal" colonial division of labor and "unequal" ecological exchanges, which divided the social actors of the world between white, Christian, civilized, and "developed" European colonizers (masters) whose "burden" was to civilize and (under) develop the "undeveloped," "backward," non-European, colonized, colored, other, "heathens" (slaves) of the world. This European civilizing of the non-European colored "heathens" of the world initially took place through the Christian churches of the West, whose biblical tenets and metaphysics were used to justify the master/slave relationship of colonialism as well as teach its work ethic, which eventually homogenized the social actions of social actors to benefit the white male power elites of an emerging gendered, racialized, and religious global capitalist world-system that developed the white colonizer, while simultaneously underdeveloping the colored colonized who were systematically forced to become agents of the Protestant ethic in agricultural production. A hybrid administrative bourgeoisie, and the poor seeking to be like them, emerged among the colonizers.

The end of the socioeconomic military colonial system in the form of decolonization in the twentieth century did not end the colonizer/colonized relational relationship, but gave rise to a new nation-state system of civilizing, domination, and exploitation within the hegemony of this emerging gendered, racialized, and religious global capitalism. Decolonization gave birth to what Philip McMichael calls, "the development project." According to McMichael, "[t]he mid-twentieth century development project (1940s-1970s), an internationally orchestrated program of national economic growth, with foreign financial, technological, and military assistance under the conditions of the Cold War, managed the aftermath of collapsing European and Japanese empires within the idealistic terms of the United nations and its focus on [national-state] governments implementing a human rights-based social contract with their citizens. . . to equalize conditions across the world in laying the foundations of a global market that progressively overshadowed the states charged with development in the initial post-World War II era" (McMichael, 2008, pg. 21). Hence, the development project from the postcolonial era to the 1970s emphasized and continued the "unequal" colonial division of labor and "unequal" ecological exchanges within an Ameri-centric dominated capitalist world-system subdivided into three geopolitical segments to benefit capitalist accumulation: the First World, the developed capitalist Western countries plus Japan with America the model for development; the Second World comprised of Communist Soviet blocs; and the Third World comprised of postcolonial bloc of nations.

Whereas under colonialism, as McMichael notes, "[t]he basic pattern was to establish in the colonies specialized extraction and production of raw materials and primary products that were unavailable in Europe. In turn, these products fueled European manufacturing as industrial inputs and foodstuffs for its industrial labor force" (31), in the development phase of postcolonial capitalism, the process was reversed as the First World sought to take advantage of the desire of the postcolonial elites, the administrative bourgeoisie, of the Third World to develop their nation-states along the lines of the industrial First World. The basic global pattern was to establish in the emerging postcolonial "Third-World" nation-states specialized manufacturing and industrial production sites that were outsourced from the First World. In turn, the outsourcing of these manufacturing and industrial jobs by the First World to take advantage of the urban underemployment and low-wage economy caused by the de-agriculturalization of Third World countries fueled First World, especially American, agribusinesses that channeled food surpluses, under a "food-aid-regime," to Third World countries. "In agriculture, the Third World's share of world agricultural exports fell from 53 to 31 percent between 1950 and 1980, while the American granary consolidated its critical role in world agricultural trade. By the 1980s, the United States was producing 17 percent of the world's wheat, 63 percent of its corn, and 63 percent of its soybean; its share of world exports was 36 percent in wheat, 70 percent in corn, and 59 percent in soybeans" (McMichael, 2008, pgs. 67-68).

What developed from this global economic relationship was that Third World industrialization outlined by W.W. Rostow's stages of development fueled First world economic growth agriculturally and technologically, while underdeveloping some Third World countries, and dependently developing others within the capitalist global world-system, hence recolonizing the Third World as they became indebted given their need to import food to feed their populous.

The postcolonial nations had no say in this new "unequal" development paradigm as "decisions about postcolonial political arrangements were made in London and Paris where the colonial powers, looking to sustain spheres of influence, insisted on the nation-state as the only appropriate political outcome of decolonization" (McMichael, 2008, pg. 47). Be that as it may, "[t]his new paradigm inscribed First World power and privilege in the new institutional structure of the postwar international economy. In the context of the Cold War between First and Second Worlds (for the hearts and resources of the ex-colonial world), "development" was simultaneously the restoration of a capitalist world market to sustain First World wealth, through access to strategic natural resources, and the opportunity for Third World countries to emulate First World civilization and living standards" (McMichael, 2008, pg. 45). The "development project," in this way, as McMichael further observed, continued the hegemony of capitalism, which started with colonialism, through the universalization of a global market system driven by the nation-state and economic growth through agricultural and industrial productions (2008, pg. 46). Globalization (1970s-2000s) is a continuation of this hegemonic capitalist process in a post-communist world.

Globalization under American capitalist hegemony seeks to dismantle the state-centered exploitation of colonial and development capitalism via the invisible hand of economic (neo) liberalism, education, class division, and social relations of global production. "The globalization project (1970s-2000s)," as McMichael observes, "liberalizing trade and investment rules, and privatizing public goods and services, has privileged corporate rights over the social contract and redefined development as a private undertaking" (2008, pg. 21). That is to say, in reestablishing a global capitalist economy through the development project that followed colonialism, the First World was able to indebt Third World countries through an export-oriented industrialization that fueled the wealth of First World agribusinesses, transnational corporations, and their citizens who became consumers of inexpensive manufactured goods from the Third World. Hence, "[e]xport-oriented industrialization fueled rapid economic growth, legitimizing a new 'free market' model of development, and in the 1980s this was represented as the solution to the debt crisis [of Third World countries]. Development, which had been defined as nationally managed economic growth, was redefined in the World Bank's *World Development Report 1980* as 'participation in the world market'" (McMichael, 2008, pg. 117). This global market is controlled and directed by multinational and transnational corporations operating in First World postindustrial cities where high finance banking jobs and low-end service jobs predominate over manufacturing and industrial jobs that have been outsourced to semi-periphery or developing nations. What has developed in turn is a continuation of the tripartite system of the development phase. In the globalization phase, however, what has developed is a tripartite system in which the global economic system parallels Immanuel Wallerstein's world-systems conception: a periphery group of poor nations whose comparative advantage are raw materials, agricultural production, and tourism; a semi-periphery group of industrial based nations, i.e., India, Mexico, Brazil, South Africa, and China; and a postindustrial group of core or developed nations led by the United States of America who generate profit by servicing the cultural consumptive needs of a multicultural and multiethnic transnational capitalist class who control and monitor their (US and other core countries) investments in periphery and semi-periphery nations.

In other words, the contemporary (1970 to the present) post-industrial mode of production in developed (core) states like the US is no longer characterized or driven by the industrial means for accumulating capital, which dominated the social relations of production of the last one hundred years in core or developed nations. Instead, the present globalization condition is driven-by, post-industrialism (consumerism)—the new means for accumulating capital—, and in such "developed" societies like the U.S., is characterized not by the industrial organization of labor, which have been outsourced overseas, but rather by capitalist finance and service occupations catering to the consumerist demands of a dwindling (transnational, transcultural, transracial, etc.) middle class the world over. In short, the rate of economic gain for its own sake or profit has fallen in industrial production due to labor laws (products of the welfare state) and ecological cost in developed countries like the US; hence the practice now among investors operating out of the US and other developed nations is on financial expansion "in which 'over-accumulated' capital switches from investments in production and trade, to investments in finance, property titles, and other claims on future income" (Trichur, 2005, pg. 165).

On a global scale, the bifurcation defining this current conjuncture is characterized on the one hand by an expansion of industrial production into some (others remain agricultural producers) developing or periphery countries, i.e., the semi-periphery, where the rate of labor exploitation has risen given their lack of environmental and labor laws, devalued labor, and the dismantling of the welfare state; and on the other hand, consumerism of cheaply produced goods and high-end service occupations has come to dominate developed and developing societies as capital in the developed world seeks to allow and incorporate, through the commodification of their cultural identities, the transnational class of elite "others" who administer the assets of capital into their consumption patterns. Archer et al (2007) sum up the nature of this position brilliantly,

> since the mid-1990s, the application of GATS ([General Agreement on Trade in Services)] has slowly but surely led to a redefinition of culture primarily if not exclusively within the parameters of neo-liberal capitalism. The presumption is that flourishing cultures go hand-in-glove with flourishing capitalism. . . .[t]his strategic articulation and subordination of culture to the requirements of capitalism is what has been called 'cultural capitalism'. . . .This line of thinking is best exemplified by David Harvey. . . and to a lesser extent by Fredric Jameson. . . himself. These theorists have launched an unrelenting critique of cultural capitalism as a 'carnival for the elite' which enables politicians and policymakers to conceal growing socio-spatial inequalities, polarizations, and distributional conflicts between the haves and the have-nots. This critique is further underscored by their dismissal of culture as nothing more than a tool for economic regeneration through the 'mobilization of the spectacle'. . . , because the tourist and entertainment city requires the urban spectacle to reinforce place-marketing and residential development. . . .In short, for this group, culture is just another commodity available for consumption in the world's supermarkets (3).

"Globalization-as-culture" theorists out rightly reject this socioeconomic position or interpretation underlying the processes of globalization. They believe "that globalization is marked by the hollowing out of national cultural spaces either consequent upon the retrenchment of the nation state or because culture continues to be a relatively autonomous sphere" (Archer et al, 2007, pg. 2). That is, "[f]or the "globalization-as-culture" group. . . culture is not that easily enjoined due to its inherent counter-hegemonic properties vis-à-vis neo-liberal globalization. Rather, for this group. . . , contemporary globalization is not merely economic, but a system of multiple cultural articulations which are shaped by disjunctive space-time coordinates. In other words, globalization is as much if not more the product of inexorable and accelerated migratory cultural flows and electronic mass mediations beyond the space-time envelopes of the nation-state system and the successive socio-spatial fixes of global capitalism" (Archer et al, 2007, pg. 4). In fact, culture, in many instances, serves as a counter-hegemonic movement to (neo) liberal capitalism as a governing "rational" system. This line of thinking is best exemplified in the works of Stuart Hall (1992), John Tomlinson (1999), Homi Bhabha (1994), and Edward Said (1993) among many (postcolonial) others. For these theorists cultural exchanges are never one-dimensional, and hybridization of culture in many instances serves as a counter-hegemonic force to the homogenization processes of global capital.

Theoretically, this debate between the advocates of the "globalization-as-culture" and the "culture-of-globalization" hypotheses is a fruitless debate grounded in a false ontological and epistemological understanding regarding the origins and nature of the (neo) liberal capitalist system that gives rise to the processes of globalization. Both groups ontologically and epistemologically assume that the origins of capitalism and its discursive practice is grounded in reason and rationality, thus drawing on the liberal distinction between capitalism as a public and neutral system of rationality that stands apart from the understanding of it as a private sphere or lifeworld cultural form grounded in the ontology of the Protestant ethic as argued by Max Weber. The latter position, if assumed by both schools, is a point of convergence that resolves their opposition, and gives a better understanding of the origins and nature of the processes of globalization and counter movements to what are in fact metaphysical cultural forces/social class language games.

Both schools of thought are putting forth the same convergence argument, the culture of globalization position from a Marxian systems integration perspective and the globalization as culture position from a Weberian social integration perspective. For the culture of globalization position cultural practices are homogenized to be integrated within the rational rules or systemicity/social class language game of capitalist relations of production and consumption at the world-system level so as to generate surplus-value from the consumption of cultural products as commodities in core postindustrial nations, industrial production in semi-periphery nations, and agricultural production in periphery nations.

The globalization as cultural group suggests that in the process of acculturating social actors to the organization of work within the capitalist world-system, homogenization does not take place. Instead, in the process of integration within the world-system, cultural groups, present-at-hand, intersubjectively defer meaning in ego-centered communicative discourse to hybridize the lexicons of significations coming out the globalization process thereby maintaining their cultural forms not in a commodified form but as a class-for-itself seeking to partake in the global community as hybrid social actors governed by the liberal rational logic of the marketplace.

The two positions are not mutually exclusive, however. Within my phenomenological structural logic, globalization contemporarily represents the homogenization of social discourse and action via hybridization. That is globalization represents the discursive practice, "spirit of capitalism," social class language game of agents of the Protestant Ethic seeking to allow for and homogenize "other" human behaviors, cultures, around the globe within the logic of their metaphysical discourse, "The Protestant Ethic and the spirit of capitalism social class language game," so as to accumulate profit, via agricultural, industrial, and post-industrial/consumerist production, for the predestined from the damned on a global scale. That is, via globalization social actors around the globe are interpellated and socialized or embourgeoised via ideological apparatuses, churches, education, prisons, class division, and social relations of production, to become agents of the Protestant ethic so as to fulfill their labor and consumption roles in the organization of work, agricultural, industrial, or postindustrial production, required by their states in the global capitalist world-system under American hegemony since World War II. Proper socialization in the contemporary capitalist American dominated world-system is tantamount to hybridization, i.e., a liberal bourgeois Protestant *other* working for those who own the means and forces of production so as they themselves can become bourgeois as profit trickles down from capital operating in the first world or developed countries to the rest of the world, in order to consume the cultural and individual products found in postindustrial world-cities throughout the globe. Hence, hybridization of other cultures, via the homogenization process of globalization, is a simulacrum of white agents of the Protestant ethic, which enables the latter (whites) to make social actors of other cultures known for two reasons, to socialize them to the work ethic of the globalizing process and to accumulate surplus-value as the former service the others of their community for what has become since the 1960s a multicultural, multisexual, multiracial, etc., global capitalist world-system dominated by whites and hybrid others, who unready-to-hand (because the discriminatory effects of the society prevented them from doing so under slavery, colonial, etc.) sought during colonization to partake in the Protestant capitalist social structure for equality of opportunity, recognition, and distribution with their white counterparts. As previously highlighted, the créolité, hybridity, ambivalence, etc., language of postmodern, post-structural, and postcolonial discourses represent the concepts, pathologies, etc., of the once-discriminated against "other" as they seek equality of opportunity, recognition, and distribution with their former slave-masters and colonizers by recursively reorganizing and reproducing their ideas and ideals as an "other."

Haiti would become constituted as a republic between the hybrid mulatto elites and educated petit-bourgeois blacks (collectively known here as the Affranchis), dialectically, seeking, unready-to-hand, to be agents of the Catholic/Protestant Ethic and the spirit of capitalism for equality of opportunity, recognition, and distribution with whites, and the Haitian masses who were and are not a structurally differentiated other, i.e., poor black underclass. On the contrary, they were and are, unlike other blacks in America and the diaspora, structuralized or interpellated and ounganified/manboified within the language, ideology, ideological apparatuses, and communicative discourse of *oungan yo*, *manbo yo, gangan yo*, and *granmoun yo* who recursively reorganized and reproduced a different form of system and social integration, the Vodou Ethic and the spirit of communism, on the island against the former, the Catholic/Protestant Ethic and the spirit of capitalism social class language of the whites and Affranchis.

NOTES

1. Here, once again, I am using the African/Taino/Haitian Kreyol language for priests, priestesses, healers, and elders.

2. The prosperity gospels of the Protestant churches in contemporary America go hand in hand with the conspicuous consumptive logic of its postindustrial mode of production. Whereas frugality and accumulative wealth once dominated the Protestant Ethic, today the emphasis is on hard work and material wealth as a sign of God's grace and blessings, which feeds the consumptive logic of postindustrial finance capital.

Chapter Four

A Phenomenological Structural Constitution of Haitian Society

"The Vodou Ethic and the Spirit of Communism"

If the constitution of European society is a by-product of their ready-to-hand, unready-to-hand, and present-at-hand constitution and reification, via the nation-state and its ideological apparatuses, of their brutal ecological existence, the Northern Cradle-Greek Model, as the Protestant Ethic and the spirit of capitalism language game, which they universalized and reified with the nature of reality as such, and have sought to export (globalization) throughout the world since the seventeenth century. The majority of black consciousnesses, as a result of slavery, racism, and colonization, in Africa and the diaspora are an unready-to-hand, ready-to-hand, and present-at-hand, dialectical response to their marginalization within this reified worldview. In other words, the majority of blacks in Africa and the diaspora are "other" agents of the Protestant Ethic, a comprador bourgeoisie in the words of Frantz Fanon (1963, 1967), seeking, unready-to-hand and present-at-hand, as a result of their marginalization within slavery and the colonial system, to recursively reorganize and reproduce, as an "other," the tenets of the Protestant Ethic and the spirit of capitalism for equality of opportunity, recognition, and distribution with their white counterparts amidst the existence of a structurally differentiated black underclass of their societies.'

Given their interpellation, embourgeoisement, and differentiation via the language, ideology, ideological apparatuses, and modes of production of the West, this structurally differentiated black underclass does not have an alternative practical consciousness from the comprador bourgeoisie. Instead, they are structurally differentiated by the rules of conduct that are sanctioned by the Protestant Ethic and the spirit of capitalism as implemented by the black comprador bourgeoisie through the language, Protestant Ethic ideology, ideological apparatuses such as schools, army, police force, the church, prisons, etc., the mode of production (agribusinesses, tourism, and manufacturing), and communicative discourse as prescribed by whites.

Contrarily, the majority of Haitian practical consciousness is a ready-to-hand and present-at-hand anti-dialectical response to such a worldview as it stands against the unready-to-hand, ready-to-hand, and present-at-hand Catholic/Protestant Ethic and the spirit of capitalism of the *Affranchis* and European minorities on the island.[1] Like the rest of the black/African diaspora, in Haiti the administrative or comprador bourgeoisie, Affranchis, would develop prior to, during, and following the Revolution. However, the majority of the Africans of the "maroon republics" in the provinces and mountains of Haiti were not a structurally differentiated black other as one would find throughout the diaspora. On the contrary, they were subjects/agents of an alternative form of system and social integration, the Vodou Ethic and the spirit of communism social class language game. The originating moments of the Haitian Revolution as initiated on August 14th, 1791 at Bois Caïman by Boukman Dutty, Cecile Fatiman, and Edaïse was led by Africans under the, present-at-hand, leadership of *oungan yo, manbo yo, gangan yo*, and *granmoun yo*, anti-dialectically, seeking to constitute and recursively (re) organize and reproduce their African Kreyol and Vodou practical-consciousness, the Vodou Ethic and the spirit of communism social class language game, in the world via its Vodou ideology (*konesans*); modes of productions, i.e., subsistence agriculture, husbandry, and komes; and ideological apparatuses, i.e., Lakous, peristyles, *lwa yo*, herbal medicine and healers (*gangan/dokté féy*), Vodou magic and rituals, *vévés*, songs, dances, musical instruments, proverbs, secret societies, i.e., Bokor, Bizango, Sanpwel, lougawou, and zombification, which stood against the bourgeois Catholic/Protestant liberalism of whites and the mulatto/petit-bourgeois blacks or Affranchis class of Haiti (Genovese, 1979; Fick, 1990). The latter would subsequently, with the assassination of the *oungan,* Vodou priest, Jean-Jacques Dessalines on October 17th, 1806, undermine that attempt for a more dialectical liberal purposive-rationale, similar to that of the rest of the administrative bourgeoisie of the black diaspora. Their (Affranchis) failure to effectively establish ideological apparatuses in the provinces and the mountains to interpellate and embourgeois the masses as agents of the Catholic/Protestant Ethic and the spirit of capitalism against the mode of production, ideology, ideological apparatuses, and communicative discourse of the Vodou Ethic and the spirit of communism of *oungan yo, manbo yo, gangan yo,* and *granmoun yo*, however, undermined their attempt to reproduce the nation-state as a simulacrum of European/French society. Albeit they would subsequently work with foreign white merchants, within the capitalist world-system, to underdeveloped the provinces and mountains by undermining the subsistence agricultural, husbandry, and *komes* of the Africans through taxation and importation of cheap foreign goods, and silencing their history and historical narratives via the postmodern, post-structural, and postcolonial logic of syncretism, créolité, hybridity, ambivalence, and négritude (Trouillot, 1995; Bellegarde-Smith and Michel, 2006; Du Bois, 2012).

The African people of Haiti have resisted. This resistance by the majority of the African Haitians to their interpellation, embourgeoisement, and structural differentiation within the Catholic/Protestant Ethic and spirit of capitalism of the *Affranchis* is not reactionary, but a product of their Vodou Ethic and the spirit of communism social class language game, which they rationalized with the nature of reality as such. I am not suggesting, as Joan Dayan (1998) in *Haiti, History, and the Gods* claims, that the Haitian belief system of Vodou and its practices, i.e., the spirit of communism, reciprocity, justice, etc., are less a product of African survivals than of the colonial past and the history that past keeps generating. Against this postmodern, post-structural, and postcolonial appropriation of the Haitian/African belief system/practical consciousness to demonstrate créolité, ambiguity, hybridity, and liminality, and as such the subversive and resistant agency of the Haitian/Taino/Africans, I posit, in sociological parlance, a Weberian/historical-materialist constitution of the belief-system, what I call in the previous chapters phenomenological structuralism. My position highlights the ready-to-hand and present-at-hand African materialist constitution, reification, and dissemination (through its own language, ideology, ideological apparatuses, mode of production, and communicative discourse, i.e., social class language game, which Western society and the *Affranchis* tried to destroy and supplant with their own under slavery, colonialism, and the ideological apparatuses of the *post*colonial, neoliberal, system) of Haitian practical consciousness in the provinces and mountains as the Vodou Ethic and the spirit of communism.

In other words, the constitution of Haitian society, in the provinces and mountains," the maroon republics," has been a ready-to-hand intent by the majority of the Africans to recursively reorganize and reproduce their Southern-cradle Egyptian culture/civilization or language game, the Vodou ethic and the spirit of communism undergirded by the present-at-hand position of the power elites, *oungan yo, manbo yo, bokor yo, gangan yo,* and *granmoun yo* (elders) of the provinces and mountains, against the liberal bourgeois Catholic/Protestant language game of Europeans and the *Affranchis* of the island operating through the state and its ideological apparatuses. The Affranchis, ineffectively, attempted to curtail, through the language, ideology, ideological apparatuses, and communicative discourse of the state, the development of the Vodou Ethic and the spirit of communism as a system, even though it is constituted as a form of system/social integration in the provinces, mountains, and urban slums of the island.[2]

As a result of their failed attempts, two structuring structures (system/ social integration) emerged in Haiti prior to, during, and following the Revolution, the former, the Catholic/Protestant Ethic and the spirit of capitalism social class language game, in the urban centers and the latter, the Vodou Ethic and the spirit of communism social class language game, in the maroon republics of the provinces and mountains. That is, the constitution of Haitian society in the provinces and mountains is the by-product of the structuralizing and differentiating effects of the Vodou ethic and the spirit of communism—via subsistence agricultural mode of production, husbandry, commerce (*komes*); the Kreyol language; Vodou ideology (*konesans*); and its ideological apparatuses, i.e., Lakous (Vodou family compounds), peristyles (Vodou temples), communal living (communism), *lwa yo*, herbal medicine, healers, songs, dance, etc., initially—under the leadership of religious African men and women, *oungan yo* (priests), *Bokor yo* (sorcerers), *gangan yo/dokté fey* (healers), and *Manbo yo* (priestesses), of Bois Caiman, "maroon republics," who institutionalized it both as a form of system and social integration. They rejected the class division and social relations of production of the Catholic feudal and Protestant capitalist orders established by the French, Americans, and the *Affranchis* on the island. In its place, *Oungan yo* (priests), *Bokor yo* (sorcerers), *Manbo yo* (priestesses), *gangan yo* (healers), and *granmoun yo* (elders) recursively reorganized and reproduced their linguistic systems, Vodou ideology, its ideological apparatuses, mode of production, and communicative discourse in a national position of their own in order to interpellate and socialize or ounganified/manboified the masses as agents/subjects of the Vodou Ethic and the spirit of communism worldview in the material world against the Catholic/Protestant bourgeois liberalism of the *Affranchis* and their European counterparts.

I am not suggesting that the Africans who met at Bois Caiman syncretized their African Vodou practical consciousness with that of the Europeans, and the ambiguity, hybridity, and liminality of that syncretism provided them the space to speak as subalterns. That is the position of the Affranchis, contemporarily, who, ambivalently, seek to creolize, hybridize, etc., the African worldview not as a form of system/social integration but as a commodity form to generate economic gain and equality of opportunity, recognition, and distribution with whites within the capitalist world-system under American hegemony. Conversely, at Bois Caiman, the representatives of the African "maroon republics" rejected the European worldview or social class language game and *oungan yo, manbo yo, bokor yo, gangan yo*, and *granmoun yo* (elders) syncretized their African worldviews with native Taino traditions, which paralleled the Congo African traditions. They reified and sought to institutionalize it in the material world via the language of Kreyol; the ideology and ethic (*konesans*) of Vodou; its ideological apparatuses, Lakous, peristyles, herbal medicine, *lwa yo*, songs, dance, musical instruments, magic and rituals, and proverbs, against that of the European worldview or language game; and modes of production, subsistence agriculture, husbandry, and komes. The European worldview operated within but beneath the *les mysteres* of the Vodou Ethic and spirit of communism social class language game as prescribed by the power elites, *oungan yo, manbo yo, Bokor yo, gangan yo,* and *granmoun yo* (elders) of the communities.

Hence whereas priests, pastors, merchants, educated professionals, and landowners served as the power elites of the Catholic/Protestant Ethic and the spirit of capitalism, *oungan yo, Manbo yo, Bokor yo, gangan yo,* and *granmoun yo* of Haiti served as the power elites of the Vodou Ethic and the spirit of communism social class language game in the maroon republics of the provinces and the mountains. Through the subsistence agricultural mode of production, husbandry, and commerce (*komes*); the Kreyol language; the ideology of Vodou; and the ideological apparatuses of the Lakous (village and family compounds), peristyles (Vodou temples), herbal medicine, Vodou ceremonies, magic and rituals, secret societies, zombification, etc., they recursively (re)organized and reproduced Haitian society in the provinces and mountains around the African and Taino practical consciousness or language game of Vodou and communal living, i.e., the Vodou Ethic and the spirit of communism. This latter worldview and its parishes or regions of influence was juxtaposed against the French language, liberal bourgeois ideology, and ideological apparatuses (Catholic church, so-called modern medicine, Haitian police force) of the Haitian state under the *Affranchis* and merchant classes, the comprador bourgeoisie of Haiti, which exploited and marginalized the majority of the Haitian masses as a peasant and underclass, in order to achieve equality of opportunity, recognition, and distribution with whites (in their factories, agribusinesses, and tourism) within the global capitalist world-system. It is incorrect to assume because in many instances the Africans used images of Catholic saints to represent the *lwas/lwaes* (*lwa yo* in Kreyol) of Vodou that this was and is a syncretism or hybridization between Vodou and Catholicism (Métraux, 1958; Deren, 1972; Fick, 1990; Desmangles, 1992; Bellegarde-Smith and Michel, 2006). The images were Africanized and incorporated, present-at-hand, into Vodou by oungan yo, manbo yo, gangan yo, and granmoun yo to interpellate and ounganify/manboify the African masses leaving the plantations into the Vodou Ethic and the spirit of communism social class language game (Desmangles, 1992).

Haitians who serve *lwa yo, serviteurs of Vodou* and Haitian Catholics are cognizant of the differences between themselves. For example, the annual July 16th pilgrimage performed by Serviteurs and Catholics to *Saut D'eau/ Sodo* (Kreyol form), which is a commune and sacred waterfall located in the central department of Haiti, is a case in point. Both serviteurs and Catholics make the pilgrimage in honor of Erzulie Danthor in Vodou and the Virgin Mary in Catholicism. In many instances the same image represents both entities. But the serviteur will testify to the fact that they are going to serve manbo Erzulie Danthor, recognized as the goddess of the Haitian nation by Vodou serviteurs, and Catholics will tell you they are going to honor the Virgin Mary, who appeared at the site in the nineteenth century.

What was established in Haiti by *oungan yo, manbo yo, bokor yo, gangan yo,* and *granmoun yo* prior to, during, and following the Revolution was the Vodou Ethic and the spirit of communism language game as the supreme mystery system, which governs the universe and all social relations, including the practices of the whites which operated beneath, but within the mystery system of Vodou, which they rationalized as the nature of reality as such against the Catholic/Protestant Ethic and the spirit of capitalism of the whites and *Affranchis*. The latter, like their white counterparts before them, attempted (through their anti-superstitious campaigns), with the aid of the French clergy, Protestant Churches, and American occupying forces, to marginalize and eradicate (*dechoukaj*) the Vodou Ethic and the spirit of communism in an effort to constitute the Haitian nation-state as a so-called black Republic (Métraux, 1958; Deren, 1972; Fick, 1990; Desmangles, 1992; Bellegarde-Smith and Michel, 2006; Du Bois, 2004, 2012; Ramsey, 2014). However, thus far they have failed. Instead, as their economic policies, adopted from their former colonizers, forced many Africans off of their lands into the cities where they recursively reorganized and reproduced the Vodou Ethic and the spirit of communism in the urban slums, the Affranchis had no choice but to co-opt and incorporate it into their nation-building efforts as a commodity to entertain tourists as opposed to a form of system and social integration.

THE VODOU IDEOLOGY AND ETHIC

Like the Europeans who migrated out of Africa and experienced, ready-to-hand, a brutal existence in the barren environment of Europe, where they constituted and reified, unready-to-hand and present-at-hand, an overarching worldview via the Protestant Ethic and the spirit of capitalism that juxtaposed the world as an object that stands against their subjective existence, which it threatened. Africans, prior to their enslavement, also reified, present-at-hand, a worldview based on their initial ready-to-hand experiences of the earth. However, unlike the Europeans, the Africans encountered a bountiful environment that provided everything they needed for their physical survival in the material world. Be that as it may, they reified and constituted their being-in-the-world under an overarching worldview/language game, the Vodou Ethic and the spirit of communism social class language game, which emphasized their existence as sacred, communal, and an extension or manifestation of Bon-dye, i.e., the world-spirit, which is everywhere and in everything. The earth, which is a manifestation of Bon-dye, and its tilling and cultivation, through agricultural production, became a means of uniting with the spiritual world, which is good (*Bon-dye Bon*).

As such, for the Africans, Vodou became a monotheistic religion in which the one God, *Bon-dye*, or *Gran-Mét* (I am using the language of Haitian/African Vodou as opposed to switching back and forth to different African tribal nomenclatures for the name of God), the primeval pan-psychic field, is an energy force that gave rise to a sacred, cosmic, and geometrical world out of itself. Everything that is the world, universe, galaxies, animate and inanimate objects, etc. are a manifestation of *Bon-dye*, and are sacred. Thus, unlike the jealous and barbaric God of Judaism, Christianity, and Islam, which stands outside of spacetime and makes human beings, the fallen, the superior creation of its design, i.e., the earth, which is to be exploited and dominated for human happiness and wealth. The God of Vodou has no such place for the human being. *Bon-dye* is spacetime, and the human being is no different from any other creation that is a part of this being. The aim of the human individual is to maintain balance, harmony, and perfection between nature/God, the geometric laws of creation, the cosmic forces (which aided Bon-dye in creating the multiverse), the community, and the individual.

Out of Bon-dye, the geometric laws of creation and the cosmic forces (lwa Legba, Gede, Zaka, Damballah, and Ezili) were created to assist Bon-dye in creating the multiverse and habitable worlds. According to Vodou mythology, one of Bondye's first creations when he fashioned the world was the sun (identified with the lwa Legba in Haitian Vodou metaphysics). Without its existence, lwa yo, human beings, and all the multiplicity of things could not exist. All derive from this primordial light. In Vodou, the sun with which Legba is identified is a regenerative life-force whose rays cause the vegetation to grow and ensure the maturation and sustenance of human life. Legba is the patron of the universe, the link between the Godhead and the universe, the umbilical cord that connects the universe to its origin. Bondye fashioned the universe; Legba has nurtured it, has fostered its growth, and has sustained it. Legba is also said to be androgynous; hence, his vévé contains the symbol of his sexual completeness, and he is invoked in matters related to sex. He is the cosmic phallus. Both as phallus and as umbilical cord, Legba is the guarantor of the continuity of human generations. Just as Legba initiates time, so Gede ends time, for he is the master of Ginen who rules over death. In a sense, Gede is Legba's opponent, for whereas Legba as the sun is omnipresent during the day, Gede is lord of the night and is symbolized by the moon. Whatever, Legba conceives, Gede aborts; and whatever Legba sustains Gede destroys, for he is the lord of death, the master of destruction of things. Although these two divine forces appear to have opposite functions, and indeed are inversions of each other, they nevertheless are similar in many ways, for both participate in the creative forces at opposite ends of the spectrum of life. Damballah, the gentle snake of the primal seas is identified with eternal motion in the universe. This motion is characterized by the passage of all physical phenomena from birth to decay, and produces the physical displacement of objects in space and in time, manifests itself in the incessant motion of the waves of the ocean, the waters of springs and rivers, ensures the alternation of day and night, and impels the cyclical motion of the astral bodies. In short, Damballah is a living quality expressed in all dynamic motion in the cosmos, in all things that are flexible, sinuous, and moist, in all things that fold, and unfold, coil and recoil. In humans, this energy-force is the giver of children. It is identified not only with the eternal motion of human bodies but also with motion as seen in the cycle of life and death and in the passing of human generations. If motion is ensured by Damballah, and if, as generating principle, the phallus is symbolized by Legba and Gede, Ezili represents the cosmic womb in which divinity and humanity are conceived. She is the symbol of fecundity, the mother of the world who participates with the masculine forces in the creation and maintenance of the universe. As mother, Ezili cooperates with the sun lwa Legba, who ensures the florescence and nurture of all living things. When she cooperates with Gede, she symbolizes Ginen's cosmic womb from which the released ancestral gwo-bon-anjs are reclaimed. In combination with Damballah, Ezili guarantees the flow of human generations. Vodou mythology conceives her as the mother of the lwas and of humanity. She is believed to have given birth to the first human beings after Bondye created the world, and since that time her powers of provision have continued to grant children to the human community, a community reliant on Gede's cousin, Zaka, the cosmic lord of agriculture, who is docile, gentle, and kind (Desmangles, 1992, pgs. 108-132).

Ideologically in Vodou, therefore, as in all other West African and Native American beliefs, the human being and all that is the universe is a manifestation of *Bon-dye*. Balance, harmony, perfection, and subsistence living with this Being as revealed in nature and it's tilling, cultivation, and husbandry is the *modus operandi* for human existence. This one good God is an energy force that manifests itself in the human plane of existence via the ancestors and four hundred and one *lwa yo* (concepts, cosmic forces, and animistic spirits materialized), which humans can access as a material energy force and concepts to assist them in being-in-the-world in order to maintain the aforementioned balance, harmony, perfection, and subsistence living of Bondye. Hence, like the God of Judaism, the Good God, *Bon-dye Bon*, of Vodou is active in history and in current political events, via ancestors, *lwa yo*, and humans, rather than in the primordial sacred time of myth. Unlike the God of Judaism, however, in Vodou human beings are not distinct, fallen, from that great energy force due to sin and must, therefore, seek to reunite with it by exercising good moral conduct on earth. In the pantheistic worldview of

Vodou, the human being, like all other beings, whether sentient or not, are a manifestation of the energy force of *Bon-dye*. In other words, the human being is a spirit or energy force living in a material body or physical temple. We are constituted energy, which is recycled or reincarnated sixteen times, eight times as a male and eight times as a female, on the planet earth in order to achieve perfection (Beauvoir, 2006). There is no moral right or wrong in Vodou. "Followers define moral principles for themselves and are guided by life's lessons, the wisdom of ancestors, and communication with spirits" (Michel, 2006, pg. 34). The aim is the manifestation of the power of Bon-dye amongst the plane of human existence. As such, the energy, which consti-tutes the human being, is not punished for acts done in the material world through the descent into animal embodiment as highlighted in the reincarna-tion logic of Hinduism, Buddhism, and Jainism. The emphasis in Vodou is on experiencing the lived-world, subsistence living, and perfection. The clos-er the human being gets to their sixteenth experiences on earth and perfec-tion, the wiser and less materialist they are (which is different from the Protestant ethic which emphasizes material wealth as a sign of god's grace and predestination). At the end of their sixteenth life cycles the energy that constitutes the human being is reabsorbed with the original energy force, *Bon-dye*, the primeval pan-psychic field, which manifested them as life.

In sum, Vodou is a product of the Egyptian/Ethiopian mystery system, *les mystere*. "The entire hieroglyphic system of Egypt is based upon the symbol-ic connection which exists between the various beings [of the world] and the cosmic forces, between the beings and the *lois* [(lwa in Kreyol)] (laws of creation)" (Rigaud, 1985, pg. 11). The Vodou belief system posits that *Bon-dye*, God, is the architect of the universe, which was created via geometric laws of creation and cosmic forces. The "laws of creation" create the cosmic forces and other *lwa yo* in visible manifestations such as the planets, suns, plants, animals, and human beings within geometric spacetime. The Vodou rites are derived from the cosmic forces of the planets and suns created by the geometric laws of creation, which are recreated via the ideological appara-tuses, i.e., peristyles, dances, songs, musical instruments, magic and rituals, vévés, alters, etc., of human beings. From the cosmic forces of the planets and suns, plants, animals, and human beings were created within geometric spacetime. Nature, the ideological apparatuses, i.e., symbols, musical instru-ments, lakous, peristyles, and ounfo of human beings, and their practical consciousness must correspond to these geometric laws of creation and the cosmic forces.

As such, human beings recreate this creation via the lakous, ounfo, peri-styles, vévés, magic and rituals, personal alters (*pe*) to the cosmic forces and ancestors, agricultural production, husbandry, and komes, which in total cap-ture that creation and how humans are to live within it. As Gerdés Fleurant (2006) highlights,

[t]he primary unit of Vodun social organization is the *lakou* (compound), and extended family and socioeconomic system whose center is the *ounfo* (temple), to which is attached the *peristyle* (the public dancing space). Vodun, a danced religion, acknowledges the unity of the universe in the continuity of Bondye, or God; the Lwa, or mediating spiritual entities; humans, animals; plants; and minerals. Vodun is also a family religion in the sense that its teachings, belief systems, and rituals are transmitted mainly through the structure of the family. It has a sacerdotal hierarchy comprised of the *oungan* (male) and the *manbo* (female) and their assistants, the *laplas* (sword bearer), *ounsi kanzo* (spouses of the spirits), *oungenikon* (chorus leader), and *ountó* (drummers). In the absence of priests, the head of the family, much like a traditional paterfamilias, conducts the service. Most ceremonies take place in the *peristyle*, whose *potomitan* (center post) is believed to incarnate ancestral and spiritual forces of family and community. The people dance around the *potomitan*, which is the point of genesis of essential segments of the ritual process (pgs. 46-47).

The center post or *potomitan* of the peristyle is the solar support of the community which unites lwa yo, the earth, nature, sun, humans, plants, animals, etc. within one geometric spacetime:

the peristyle forms geometrically the following 1) the mitan, or center—the non-dimensional point; 2) the rectangle, or lengthened square; 3) the circle; 4) the triangle; 5) the straight, horizontal line; 6) the spiral; 7) the curved, horizontal line; 8) the round, vertical line; 9) the square, vertical line; 10) the perfect square; 11) the cross, or intersecting straight lines; 12) the equilateral and the isosceles triangle, formed by the beams which secure the post to the roof (Rigaud, 1985, pg. 17).

As Leslie G. Desmangles further highlights,

The principle of inversion and retrogression is fundamental to Vodou theology as well as to its rituals. . . In Vodou the relationship between the cosmic mirror and the profane reality that it represents takes the cosmographic form of the cross. In the cross, Vodouisants see not only the earth's surface as comprehended by the four cardinal points of the universe, but also the intersection of the two world, the profane world as symbolized by the horizontal line, and Vilokan as represented by the vertical line. . . The foot of this vertical line "plunges into the waters of the abyss" to the cosmic mirror where the lwas reside; there, in this sacred subtelluric city, is Africa (or Vilokan), the mythical home of Vodouisants, the place of the lwas' origin, and Ginen, the abode of the living dead. . . The point at which the two lines intersect is the pivotal "zero-point" [(non-dimensional point)] in the crossing of the two worlds. It is a point of contact at which profane existence, including time, stops, and sacred beings from Vilokan invade the peristil through the body of their possessed devotees (pgs. 104-105).

As such the peristyle is a mirror reflection and ideological constitution of the universe and all of its forces from the moment of creation to the presence:

> The four poles sustaining the structure symbolize mythologically the four cardinal points of the universe, covered by an overarching roof that represents the cosmic vault above the earth. Like the horizontal lines of the cross, the floor of the peristil symbolizes the profane world, while the vertical pole (potomitan) in the center of the peristil represents the axis mundi, the avenue of communication between the two worlds. Although the downward reach of the potomitan appears to be limited by the peristil's floor, mythologically its foot is conceived to plunge into Vilokan, the cosmic mirror. The point at which the potomitan enters the peristil's floor symbolizes the zero-point. During the ceremonies, the potomitan becomes charged with or "polluted" by the power of the lwas. Hence, before tracing the geometrical symbols of the lwas (vévés), the oungan or mambo may touch the pole, a ritual act that empowers him or her to summon the lwas into the peristil. Thereafter, like the potomitan, the oungan's (or mambo's) body becomes in itself the source of power, a repetition of the microcosmic symbol, a moving embodiment of the vertical axis around which the universe revolves (Desmangles, 1992, pg. 105).

Within the knowledge and functions of the cosmic forces and the geometric laws of creation *oungan yo, manbo yo, bokor yo,* and *gangan yo/dokté féy,* can access *lwa yo* (animistic and cosmic spirits) for wealth, healing, luck, etc. in a community based on living in harmony with nature and its laws and products of creation, which is expressed through music, dance, husbandry, tilling and cultivating the land (for medicinal and agricultural purposes), and *komes* for human sustenance and well-being. The rites and ceremonies of Vodou, "which can be seen as the reliving of the first act of creation when Bondye fashioned the world," ensure the delicate balance and harmony between Bon-dye, the cosmic forces, the geometric laws of creation, and human actions (Desmangles, 1992, pg., 152). Within this metaphysical social system, the aim of individual existence is not economic gain as a sign of God's grace and predestination, but balance, harmony, perfection, and subsistence living.

From Egypt/Ethiopia this Worldview would spread throughout the continent and the world as human beings migrated out of Africa ((Métraux, 1958; Deren, 1972; Rigaud, 1985; Diop, 1981, 1988, 1989; Desmangles, 1992; Bellegarde-Smith and Michel, 2006). As such, Vodou united all of the 101 African tribes/nations taken to the Americas, and with their encounter with the Amerindians who emigrated out of Africa tens of thousands of years prior to the slave trade the Africans recognized their mystery system (Diop, 1988, 1989; Karenga, 1993; Van Sertima, (1976 [2003]). The power elites of the different tribes/nations (Ibo, Yoruba, Congo, Nago, Mandingo, Arada, etc.) brought to Haiti during the slave trade would assemble and unite *lwa yo* into various *nanchon* (nations) grouped into two dominant *nanchon*/nations, *Rada* and *Petwo*.

THE VODOU IDEOLOGY AND THE SPIRIT OF COMMUNISM

Normally referred to as "animism," "fetishism," "paganism," "heathenism," and "black magic" in the Western academic literature, Vodou (spelled Vodun, Voodoo, Vodu, Vaudou, or Vodoun) is the oldest monotheistic religion in the world. Commonly interpreted as "Spirits" or "introspection into the unknown," Vodou is the structuring structure of the Fon people of Dahomey and other tribes of the continent (Métraux, 1958; Deren, 1972; Rigaud, 1985; Desmangles, 1992; Bellegarde-Smith and Michel, 2006). As Milo Rigaud highlights,

> The Voodoo pantheon of gods is composed of *loas* (gods) that come from all parts of Africa. Tradition has it that the term *vo-du* is drawn from the language of the Fons. Other tribes that contributed Voodoo gods were the Nago people, the Ibos, Congos, Dahomeans, Senegalese, Haoussars, Caplaous, Mandinges, Mondongues, Angolese, Libyans, Ethiopians, and the Malgaches. Moreover, the names of these tribes generally serve to designate separate Voodoo rites themselves. For example, to serve the Mondongue gods, the Mondongue rite is followed, which, although it does not differ basically and fundamentally from the other rites, nevertheless appears superficially different. To serve the Ibo gods, the Ibo rite is celebrated. And this rite too is fundamentally related to the other rites although it may appear different... Each rite has its distinctive characteristics, although all rites generally speaking arise from the same source, have the same origin, and are completely integral (1985, pg. 8).

If we assume the African origins of civilization hypothesis of Cheik Anta Diop (1981, 1988, 1989), Vodou gave rise to all of the other traditional metaphysical systems found among the early inhabitants of this planet, the animism of the native people of the Americas, Hinduism, Shintoism, Santeria, etc., which encountered the earth in bountiful conditions, as well as Judaism (In Vodou, the understanding is that Moses, who would teach the Israelites about Vodou/Judaism, was raised in Egypt as an Egyptian and trained in the Egyptian mystery system by an oungan named Ra-Gu-El Pethro or Jethro. Moses would later bastardize the system giving rise to the perversities of Judaism) (Rigaud, 1985, pg. 14). Whereas slavery, racism, and the colonization of Africa interrupted the Vodou religion and communal way of life among many people of African descent in Africa and the diaspora, the Africans of Haiti given their early freedom from slavery and the fact that the majority of them, almost sixty-seven percent of the population, were directly from Africa when the Haitian Revolution commenced were able to maintain, reorganize, and reproduce, the Vodou way of life, and its ethic, communism, in its purest form for system and social integration (Genovese, 1979; Bellegarde-Smith and Michel, 2006; Du Bois, 2004, 2012).

According to Haitian oral history, at Bois Caiman or Bwa Kay-Imam (near the Imam Boukman Dutty's house), the birthplace of the Haitian Revolution in 1791, leaders of the "maroon republics," nineteen African tribes or nations and one tribe of the Taino nation, assembled and organized a Vodou ceremony led by the oungan, Boukman Dutty, manbo Cecile Fatiman, and Edaïse to create one new nation, the Empire of Ayiti, the twenty-first tribe or nation of the ceremony, in the Americas around the Vodou religion, its ethic of democracy and communal living, and the Kreyol language. As highlighted by Boukman's prayer, the aims were to recursively reorganize and reproduce the Vodou religion and its way of life, practical consciousness, through the new Haitian empire against the European worldview or language game practiced by the Europeans and the *Affranchis*:

> *Bon Dje ki fè la tè. Ki fè soley ki klere nou enro. Bon Dje ki soulve lanmè. Ki fè gronde loray. Bon Dje nou ki gen zorey pou tande. Ou ki kache nan niaj. Kap gade nou kote ou ye la. Ou we tout sa blan fè nou sibi. Dje blan yo mande krim. Bon Dje ki nan nou an vle byen fè. Bon Dje nou an ki si bon, ki si jis, li ordone vanjans. Se li kap kondui branou pou nou ranpote la viktwa. Se li kap ba nou asistans. Nou tout fet pou nou jete potre dje Blan yo ki swaf dlo lan zye. Koute vwa la libète k ap chante lan kè nou.*

The god who created the sun which gives us light, who rouses the waves and rules the storm, though hidden in the clouds, he watches us. He sees all that the white man does. The god of the white man inspires him with crime, but our god calls upon us to do good works. Our god who is good to us orders us to revenge our wrongs. He will direct our arms and aid us. Throw away the symbol of the god of the whites who has so often caused us to weep, and listen to the voice of liberty, which speaks in the hearts of us all.

Although the usurpation of the Revolution by the Affranchis leadership, curtailed the nationalization of Vodou via the nation-state of Haiti, the power elites of the Vodou worldview were able to institutionalize and constitute it in the provinces and mountains of the island as the form of social/system integration for the masses.

Within the Vodou worldview or language game and its communal organizations and practices, serviteurs, practitioners of Vodou, as previously highlighted, believe *Bon-dye*, the primeval pan-psychic field, created the multiverse and all of its objects out of itself. As such, the earth, its objects, and all life on it are a manifestation of *Bon-dye* through our *nanm* (soul), and as such are sacred. Bon-dye manifests itself in the material and spiritual, or energy world, through the spiritual and conceptual essences of the four hundred and one *lwa yo* and deceased ancestors (*lwa rasin* or *lwa eritaj*) (ancestor worship is huge in Haiti), who manifest themselves to the living in dreams, divinations, and bodily possessions so that they can maintain balance and harmony within the material world, which is the manifestation of Bon-dye. *Lwa yo*, in essence, are manifestations of Bon-dye who exist, without a material body, in a different dimension of spacetime from living human beings as energy. Because the energy force of Bon-dye is so vast and powerful, it manifests itself in the material world through the deceased ancestors and *Lwa yo*, who represent cosmic forces, concepts, values, and personalities for us to model in the material world in order to achieve balance, harmony, subsistence living, and perfection as we experience being-in-the-world. Although they do not possess corporeal bodies, *lwa yo* nonetheless have personalities and enjoy corporeal things such as drinking, eating, smoking, dancing, and talking.

Lwa yo, essentially, are cosmic forces, the spirits of the ancestors, and the major forces or concepts of the universe, i.e., beauty, good, evil, health, reproduction, death, and other aspects of daily life. Each *Lwa* is represented by a hieroglyphic symbol, a hieroglyphic *vévé*, and are predominantly divided into two nations or families, *Rada* and *Petwo Lwa yo*, representing *lwa yo* of the twenty-one nations of Bois Caiman. The Rada *Lwa yo* are relatively peaceful, happy spirits, cosmic forces, and concepts, beauty, reproduction, etc., of daily life served by *oungan yo* and *manbo yo*. *Petwo Lwa yo* represent malevolent spirits of animals and other forces of nature, and are usually served by members, Bókós/Bokors, of secret societies to gain wealth, political power, do harm, kill, or cripple. Bokors (Bokor yo, plural form in Kreyol) are also the police force of the society or village life, and mitigate the harshest punishment, zombification, in Vodou.

The Rada traditions constitute ninety-five percent of Vodou practices, and Petwo five percent. Notwithstanding its sacerdotal hierarchy, Vodou is very democratic. Once initiated, everyone establish their lakous and peristyles and serve their *lwa* or *lwa yo* according to the will and desires of *lwa yo* (This is similar to the Protestant faith, where pastors establish their own churches based on their readings and interpretations of the bible). Albeit, recently, January, 2008, all the lakous and peristyles have organized themselves under one political organization *Konfederasyon Nasyonal Vodou Ayisyen* (KNVA) led by, Max Beauvoir, who is called the *ATI-oungan* of Vodou.

Whereas in the Petwo tradition the human individual seeks assistance from *lwa yo* through a bokor for wealth, power, i.e., *pwen*, to do harm to someone, vindicate oneself, revenge, etc., in the Rada tradition, that is not normally the case. In the Rada tradition, the human individual does not seek *lwa yo*. (Albeit, they can seek certain *Lwa* to assist them in acquiring wealth, love, health, political power, revenge, etc. But this is done through Bokors (sorcerers), initiates of secret societies in Vodou). Each person has a spiritual court, meaning that particular spirits show interest in them and become intertwined in their lives. Everyone's spiritual court is different and people must learn to recognize their spirits so they can effectively work with them. Since it can be difficult to decipher exactly what a spirit wants and which spirit is affecting a person's life, religious professionals or the power elites of Vodou, i.e., *oungan yo, Manbo yo, Bokor yo, gangan yo,* and *granmoun yo* (elders) in the family are consulted to decipher the spiritual court of an individual and ensure that their life is being led in harmony with the desires and wills of *lwa yo* who constitute their spiritual court. Once an individual's spiritual court is determined through a card reading or Vodou ceremony, many people use this knowledge to create a home altar to strengthen their relationship between themselves and *lwa yo* of their spiritual court. For individuals who are called further, they may choose to have a head washing (*lave tét*), which connects them permanently to their *mét tét* (ruler of the head) who is the spirit most closely aligned with them. The next step, if one chooses, would be to initiate into the religion into one of three stages: *ounsi* (congregation member), *manbo* or *oungan* (priestess or priest), and *manbo asogwe* or *oungan asogwe* (high priestess or high priest). These levels of initiation (*kanzo*) are not decided by the individual but by the spirits and revealed through dreams, card readings, and other forms of communication. This is a permanent life-time commitment and each level requires different duties to spirit and community. Contact provides a way to mitigate relationships with *lwa yo* and ancestors who otherwise could impact lives without individuals having the ability to negotiate their situation. *Lwa yo* and ancestors have individual personalities and preconceived notions about proper behaviors that can cause them to help or hinder people as they see fit. Engaging with *lwa yo* allow humans to gain their aid and take control over their own luck. However, this usually requires a pledge of either a direct exchange of offerings for services or a lifelong commitment to serve and honor. Failure to uphold a person's end of the deal or to recognize when a spirit is making a demand can result in punishment that affects luck, health, personal relationships, and financial situations. *Lwa yo* also become part of an extended spiritual/material family, and as such individuals love them and provide offerings because they enjoy making the Lwa yo and ancestors happy. Home altars, as in Hinduism, dedicate a space to honoring and feeding *lwa yo* and ancestors, dreams bring messages, and daily experiences reinforce their presence. Hence humans and spirit beings exist in a symbiotic relationship on earth.

Within this symbiotic relationship on earth, the Petwo tradition dialectically balances and harmonizes nature, the community, and the individual by counterbalancing the relatively peaceful and happy spirits or concepts of the Rada traditions with the malevolent forces and concepts of nature. In the Petwo tradition, the individual seeks the aid of a Bokor for wealth, political power, protection, or to do harm to an adversary through the aid of the malevolent forces or concepts, i.e., revenge, greed, hate, violence, etc., of nature. Whereas the killing, harming, etc. of an individual is not allowed in the Rada tradition, they are sanctioned in the Petwo tradition. The Petwo tradition houses both the secret societies of Vodou, which are in place to protect the society from those who violate the norms of the *ounfo*, and the sorcerers, bokors, who use their knowledge of *les mystere* to kill, cripple, or do harm (financially, socially, politically, etc.) to an individual. According to Max Beauvoir, the late *ATI-oungan* of Haitian Vodou, the Bokors stem from the Taino tradition, which paralleled the Congo elements of the Africans, of the island, and when serving in the capacity as the protector of social norms and social relations, practitioners, Bokors, of the Petwo tradition must obtain the consent of leaders, *oungan yo avek manbo yo*, of the Rada tradition, of the *ounfo*, which is not the case when serving as sorcerers to benefit themselves or those seeking power, wealth, or to do harm to an adversary. In the former instance, zombification is the ultimate punishment allowed by *oungan yo avek manbo yo* to be meted out by a bokor for violation of social norms and relations, which are deemed sacred. In the latter instance anything and everything goes, i.e., financial, social, and political ruin, zombification, or death. The Petwo tradition is consider the black magic of Vodou, and it is this tradition and its practice of zombification that is and has been portrayed by Hollywood and Wade Davis's (1985) work, *The Serpent and the Rainbow*. Conceptually, the Vodou tradition is not one or the other it is both. The two traditions represent the energy/material symbiotic (binary) world that is Bon-dye and within which all life is constituted and experiences existence.

As the *ATI-oungan* of Vodou, Max Beauvoir (2006), highlights, within this energy/material symbiotic relationship, the human being is a sentient being, which is constituted as three distinct entities, the physical body, the *gwo bon anj* (*sé médo*), and the *ti bon anj* (*sé lido*). The latter two constitute our *nanm* (soul), and the physical body is aggregated matter that eventually dies and rots. It is animated by the energy force of *Bon-dye* or the universe, the *gwo bon anj*, which is not active in influencing personality or the choices that the human subject makes in life. Instead, it is simply the spark of life or the energy force that keeps the body living or activated. In other words, metaphorically speaking, imagine the body as an electrical cord, Bon-dye as the socket, and the spark of energy from the socket that animates the appliance as the *gwo bon anj*.

The animated body, the physical body and the *gwo bon anj*, gives rise to consciousness and the personality through the *ti bon anj*. The most important part of the body is the head, which is the seat of consciousness and the space where sight, hearing, smell, and taste all reside. The five senses of the head, and the brain's reflection on what is smelled, heard, seen, tasted, and touched gives rise to the *ti bon anj*, which is consciousness, intellect, reflection, memory, will, and the personality. That is to say, it is the *ti bon anj* that houses the ego, self, personality, and ethics of the person from experiences in life. So the *gwo bon anj* animates the physical body, which gives rise to the *ti bon anj*, i.e., the individual ego or I of a human subject as they experience being in the world with others.

The three aforementioned distinct entities constitute the average individual and can be separated at various points throughout their life cycle and at the time of death. As previously mentioned, people who are called to work with *lwa yo* also have a fourth entity, personal lwa, *mét tét*, who permanently resides within their head, i.e., a sort of split personality that guides the individual in making important and daily decisions. For the average individual, at the time of death the physical body dies and rots, the *ti bon anj*, the ego, personality, etc., returns to *Ginen* (Africa), and the *gwo bon anj* lingers around seeking to animate a new body. Serviteurs, *oungan yo, Manbo yo*, and *Bokor yo*, can work to bring the *ti bon anj* of elders back across the waters from Africa so that they can be an active and honored ancestor. This latter process of ancestor retrieval is usually done a day and a year after the death of the person, and requires an animal sacrifice, i.e., the taking of a life to feed lwa yo in order to retrieve the deceased ancestor from Ginen. Upon retrieval, the *ti bon anj* of the ancestor is kept in a *govi*, a small clay bottle. Bokors, who are members of secret societies in Vodou, and stand apart from *oungan yo* and *Manbo yo* as sorcerers who serve Petwo *lwa yo*, can also capture the lingering *ti bon anj* to do spiritual work aimed at healing, ascertaining money, love relationships, work , political power, i.e., *pwen*, or other desires. This latter act is one form of zombification wherein the *ti bon anj* of a deceased person is captured in a bottle, *govi*, in directed to serve either the Bokor or an individual seeking wealth, love, political power, or to do harm to another person, etc.

Aside from separation in death, separation can also take place during a person's life cycle. During a person's life cycle, the *gwo bon anj* can be displaced by a *lwa* during possession or a Bokor for zombification. The *lwa* utilizes the animated body (the person possessed is called a *chawl* or horse for the lwa) to experience the world, heal, protect, etc. The *ti bon anj* can be displaced during a person's life cycle by a Bokor for the mitigation of punishment through zombification. This latter action is essentially the death penalty in Vodou when individuals morally violate nature, communal life, or an individual. *Bokor yo* are called upon by *oungan yo* and *manbo yo* to punish the transgressor through the removal of their *ti bon anj* from their bodies. During this process, the ego and personality, *ti bon anj*, is removed, and the person is left with the material body and the *gwo bon anj*. The purpose of this act is to render the transgressor without the desire and drive to commit any further acts, which arose from their *ti bon anj*. The person is not killed, but the desire and passion that caused them to commit the initial transgression that they committed is removed. Hence the person is left alive as a mindless zombie. Essentially, whereas oungan yo, manbo yo, and gangan/dokté fey are the readers, judges, and healers, Bokor yo are the sorcerers and police force of the village. They are practitioners of black magic, and are visited by people seeking to do harm to someone, wealth, power, luck, revenge, etc. There are three other, external, cosmic force and lwa yo that impact the individual. They are the *zetwal,* i.e., the star of a person, which determines their fate; the *lwa rasin,* or *lwa eritaj,* the spirit of the ancestors "who enter the path of the unconscious to talk to him or her in dreams, to warn of danger, and to intervene at the many levels of his [or her] life"; and the *wonsiyon,* "these are a series of spirits that accompany the *lwa mét tét* and modify somewhat the amplitude and the frequencies of its vibration or presence" (Beauvoir, 2006, pg. 128).

THE POWER ELITES, IDEOLOGICAL APPARATUSES, AND MODE OF PRODUCTION OF VODOU

The arrangements of individual, social and familial obligations, relationships, and interactions move outwards from this central cosmic, geometric, spiritual, and communal worldview or language game of Vodou, also known as the mystery system, through its power elites, oungan yo, Manbo yo, Bokor yo, gangan yo/dokté fey, and granmoun yo (elders); the agricultural mode of production, husbandry, and commerce (*komes*), which provide food for sustenance and herbs for medicinal purposes; and their ideological apparatuses, lwa yo, lakous (lakou yo), peristyles, alters, secret societies, herbal medicines, vévés, Vodou ceremonies, magic and rituals, songs, dances, musical instruments, proverbs, and zombification (Beauvoir, 2006). In Vodou, the emphasis is on balance and harmony with the laws of creation, cosmic forces, nature, the community, and within the individual all of which are interconnected. As such, agricultural production, i.e., the tilling, cultivation, and protection of the earth by men and women for food and medicinal purposes; husbandry, for food, clothing, and the making of musical instruments; and the trade (commonly referred to as commerce, *komes,* usually performed by women) of agricultural and animal products for other goods are emphasized as the proper form for human environmental, communal, and individual interactions with nature and each other. Hence initiates of Vodou are environmentally conscientious as village religious, medicinal, and agricultural life is depended on the environment, which is deemed sacred, an extension of the primeval pan-psychic field.

Village life in the majority of the provinces is constituted around the lakou, family compound, and its peristyle where everything is shared. All provinces, cities, communes in Haiti have Lakous and peristyles. The three dominant Lakous, Souvenans, Badjo, and Soukri, are located in Gonaives, Haiti and maintain the rites and traditions of Dahomey, Nago, and the Congo, respectively. The social class structure of the lakous (lakou yo) and the villages or regions they influence are not based on the mode of production but on the spiritual relationship, which is tied to nature, i.e., the sun, earth, the cycle of birth, rebirth, and death in nature. That is religious leaders and elders of the community constitute the power elites of the society followed by the middle-aged, and the young. The elders are the intermediaries between the young and the religious leaders. The functions of the religious leaders, oungan yo, manbo yo, and gangan yo/dokté féy, are healing through herbal medicine, performing Vodou ceremonies to call or pacify the spirits and bring about harmony to village life, initiating new oungan and manbo, telling the future, reading dreams, casting spells, resolving village disputes, protecting the society, and creating protections. Conversely, Bokor yo are the sorcerers and police force of the society. They are responsible for black magic, patrolling village life, through Sanpwels, Bizangos, and lougawous, and meting out punishment through zombification.

As previously mentioned, Vodou morality is not a black and white understanding of right and wrong, but rather a contextual response that above all works to maintain balance, harmony, and perfection in the universe and community. As Leslie G. Desmangles (1992) highlights,

> [v]oduisants' concepts of good and evil correspond to their idea of the forces that operate within the universe. They distinguish between good as a higher force and evil as a lower one, and correlate both with the natural order of forces in the world. A good act is of a higher order because it increases Bondye's power in the world, while a bad act is of a lower order because it decreases that power. Hence, every act, every detail of human behavior that militates against Bondye's vital force or against the increase of his power in the maintenance of order in the universe, is bad. For instance, Vodouisants consider murder wrong because, by a person's death, Bondye's divine influence is decreased in the human community. Sorcery is not wrong, because it increases the power of Bondye, as the sorcerers "tap" it from one of the lwas. The willful eradication of life is thought to be a sacrilege since it is not only a departure from Bondye's will for orderliness in the world, but an actual destruction of that order as Bondye established it (pgs. 96-97).

The universe exists in harmony as a natural state, which communal and individual life replicates, and any action that creates discord is a moral transgression. Moral transgressions are not individual acts that permanently taint the soul and change the outcome of the afterlife as one finds in Islam, Christianity, Hinduism, Buddhism, etc. There is no defined concept of heaven in Haitian Vodou and reincarnation of the *nanm* is not affected by the sins of the past life. Rather, moral transgressions change the circumstances of the individual and community in the here and now but can be overcome and moved past through some form of retribution or punishment. Also important is that the moral violation of harmony by one individual can affect the morality of the group and cause repercussions from spirits and ancestors that affect the community. This places a huge focus upon the collective and tends to downplay the individual. Yet, it would be wrong to characterize the Haitian Vodou worldview as solely a collective one. That is to say, individual action is an important part of disrupting, maintaining, and repairing balance through the religious leaders and elders of the community who must decide the appropriate course of action to take against any transgressions in order to restore balance and harmony. As the taking of life is prohibited in the Rada Vodou family, the ultimate punishment in the Haitian worldview is the second form of zombification outlined above, which is usually performed by Bokor yo of the Petwo tradition. Vodou requires that some form of retribution or punishment is required for all forms of moral transgression in order to restore balance and harmony in nature, the community, and within each individual involved in the transgression. Understandably, this is why the Haitian Revolution commences with a Petwo Vodou ceremony at Bois Caiman on August 14th, 1791. The ceremony was called upon by oungan yo, Manbo yo, Bokor yo, gangan yo, and granmoun yo (elders) under the leadership of oungan Boukman Dutty, manbo Cecile Fatiman, and Edaïse to bring about retribution and punishment against whites for the institution of slavery, which was causing great disharmony and imbalance in nature and the African communities on the island. According to Seviteurs, manbo Fatiman was mounted by the Petwo lwa, Manbo Erzulie Danthor (the lunar Goddess of the Haitian nation who the Africans summoned through the sacrifice), who meted out the punishment for the whites, and laid out the hierarchy of the leadership of the revolution. In return, as highlighted by the aforementioned Boukman's prayer, the participants promised not to serve the white man's God or allow inequality on the island. In the Vodou structuring structure, Haiti's problems are a result of the fact that they have failed to implement the covenant they made with Bon-dye (the universe) for her assistance in the form of the lunar lwa Erzulie Danthor at Bois Caiman.

Following the revolution, it would be the struggle between the modes of production, ideology, ideological apparatuses, and the agents of the two systems or structuring structures, the Vodou Ethic and the spirit of communism language game of the Africans of the provinces/mountains and the Catholic/Protestant Ethic and the spirit of capitalism language game of the *Affranchis*, mulatto elites and petit-bourgeois blacks, who were seeking to reproduce the French structuring structure in a national position of their own, which would bring about the great disharmony and imbalance that has plagued Haiti since the death of oungan Jean-Jacques Dessalines October 17th, 1806, the father of the Haitian nation, who, with his *lwa mét tét,* Ogou Feray, sought to protect the interests of those whose fathers were in Africa. Ostensibly, this struggle, contemporarily, is captured in the political discourses of political leaders and the masses as the ideas, social inclusion, democracy, equitable distribution of wealth, social wealth, social justice, etc., of the children of Dessalines vs. the ideas, i.e., capitalism, individual wealth, liberalism, etc., of the children of Pétion who assassinated him.

NOTES

1. I am not here implying that the unready-to-hand stance does not exist in the Vodou Ethic in the spirit of communism. It emerges when individuals feel that they are being punished by *lwa yo* or do not get their way in their dealings with them.

2. The anti-superstitious campaigns of the government, backed by foreign influences, are a case in point.

Chapter Five

Conclusions

The Historical Constitution of Haitian Culture or Practical Consciousnesses in an Emerging Protestant Capitalist World-System

If the African and diasporic experience as encapsulated in slavery, coloniza-tion, abolitionism, and decolonization dialectically represent the, ready-to-hand, present-at-hand, and unready-to-hand, intent of former slaves to be like their masters amidst racism, slavery, colonization, and their structural diffe-rentiation, the Africans of Haiti who met at Bois Caïman attempted to do the contrary. That is, they, anti-dialectically, rejected not only their slave status, racism, and colonization, but the very practical consciousness of their former slavemasters for their own structuring structure, i.e., the Vodou Ethic and the spirit of communism social class language game. Their discourse and discur-sive practices would eventually be supplanted by the practical consciousness or language game of the *Affranchls*, free (creole) blacks and mulatto, *gens de couleur*, bourgeoisies, seeking, like their liberal bourgeois black counterparts in America and the diaspora, equality of opportunity, distribution, and recog-nition with their *blanc* counterparts within the capitalist world-system via the Haitian state and its ideological apparatuses. Prior to this usurpation, howev-er, the Vodou and Kreyol ceremony at Bois Caïman under the leadership of Dutty Boukman, Edaïse, Cecile Fatima, the Vodou manbo priestess, is a rejection of both slave status and European civilization, and cannot be, contrary to Susan Buck-Morss's (2009) work, *Hegel, Haiti, and Universal History*, and others, conceptualized within the framework of Hegel's master/ slave dialectic, postmodern, post-structural, or postcolonial theories. Where-as the purposive-rationality of the two bourgeoisies, free landowning blacks and mulatto elites, can be conceptualized within a Hegelian dialectical, post-modern, post-structural, and postcolonial struggle, that of *oungan yo, manbo yo, gangan yo*, and *granmoun yo* of Bois Caiman, whom would assume the leadership of the masses of the provinces and mountains, cannot. The purposive-rationality of the latter was not a structurally differentiated identity. Oungan yo, manbo yo, gangan yo, and granmoun yo of Bois Caiman offered an alternative structuring structure (form of system and social integration) for organizing the material resource framework and the agential initiatives of social actors, and must not be enframed within the structurally differentiating dialectical, postmodern, post-structural, and postcolonial logic of the West and the Affranchis (today's Haitian mulatto and Arab oligarchy and petit-bourgeois blacks).

In essence, when the Haitian Revolution commences in 1791, there are three distinct groups vying for control of the island, the whites (*blancs*); free people of color and mulattoes (*Affranchis*), and the enslaved and escaped (maroon) Africans of the island. The latter, over sixty-seven percent of the population, were not a structurally differentiated other. They had their own practical consciousness, the Vodou Ethic and the spirit of communism, by which they went about recursively (re)organizing and reproducing the material resource framework. The former two, free blacks and *gens de couleur* (Affranchis), were interpellated, embourgeoised, and differentiated by the language, communicative discourse, mode of production, ideology, and ideological apparatuses of the West and shared the same European practical consciousness, the Catholic/Protestant Ethic and the spirit of capitalism social class language game. The latter stood against the Vodou Ethic and the spirit of communism social class language game of the majority of the Africans who were interpellated and ounganified/manboified by the language, communicative discourse, mode of production, ideology, and ideological apparatuses of *oungan yo, manbo yo, gangan yo*, and *granmoun yo* (James, 1986; Fick, 1990; Du Bois, 2004, 2012; Ramsey, 2014).[1]

The whites, were divided between large plantation owners, *grand blanc*, and *petit-blancs*, i.e., slave drivers, artisans, merchants, and teachers. The former, *grand blanc*, were independent-minded, and like the American colonists wanted independence from their mother-country, France, where their rights were not represented. The *petit-blancs* were more racist and feared the alliance between the larger landowners and the Affranchis. The Affranchis were free people of color and mulatto, *gens de couleur*, property and slave owners on the island who shared the religion, culture, language, and ideology of their white counterparts and wanted to remain a French colony. Although internal antagonism based on race and class existed between the free blacks and *gens de couleur*, I group them together under the nomenclature, Affranchis, to highlight the fact that their interpellation and embourgeoisement via the ideological apparatuses of the West rendered their practical conscious-

nesses identical. However, unlike the majority of white large plantation owners the majority of the Affranchis, like Vincent Ogé, André Rigaud, Pierre
Pinchinat, Toussaint Louverture, for examples, they did not want independence from France. They simply wanted their rights recognized by France,
not an independent nation-state. The enslaved and escaped Africans of the
island were divided between field slaves, domestic slaves, and maroons. The
domestic slaves, like their African-American counterparts, house slaves,
more so identified with their slavemasters. However, for the most part, the
field slaves and maroons, because of their relative isolation from whites,
domestic slaves, *gens de couleur*, and free blacks, were interpellated and
ounganified/manboified by the modes of production, language, ideology,
ideological apparatuses, and communicative discourse of the Vodou Ethic
and the spirit of communism, and sought to reproduce their African ways of
life in a national position of their own. In the end, the Revolution would
come down to a struggle between the *Affranchis* and the enslaved and maroon Africans of the island, the latter of whom commenced the Haitian
Revolution on August 14th, 1791 at Bois Caiman (Genovese, 1979; James,
1986; Fick, 1990; Du Bois, 2004, 2012). Following the Revolution, between
1804 and 1806, the purposive-rationality of the enslaved and maroon
Africans would become the *modus operandi* of the Haitian nation-state until
October 17, 1806 when Jean-Jacques Dessalines was assassinated by Alexandre Pétion and Henri Christophe. At which point, the purposive-rationality
of the *Affranchis* with their emphasis on capitalist wealth, French culture,
religion, and language became dominant at the expense of the African linguistic system, Kreyol; Vodou ideology; its ideological apparatuses; and
modes of production, subsistence agriculture, husbandry, and *komes*, of the
African masses on the island who took to the mountains and provinces following the death of Dessalines (Fick, 1990; Nicholls, 1979; Du Bois, 2004,
2012). The internal struggles between the two bourgeoisies, the mulatto elites
who controlled the export/import trade and the free blacks who controlled the
land and agribusinesses, over control of the state and its ideological apparatuses would dominate the political and economic conditions of post-revolu-
tion Haiti to the present (James, 1986; Dupuy, 1989; Fick, 1990; Nicholls,
1979; Du Bois, 2004, 2012; Buck-Morss, 2009). Both groups would arm the
youth and peasants of the island to achieve their initiatives.

PRE-REVOLUTIONARY HAITI

Contemporarily, the island which Haiti occupies in the Caribbean is inhabited by two independent nation-states: the Republic of Haiti and the Dominican Republic. Initially, the island was occupied by the Taino indigenous
people. In 1492 Christopher Columbus, seeking a Western passage to the

East Indies, claimed the island for Spain. The Spanish occupied the island and renamed it Española (written in English as Hispaniola). They exploited the island's gold mines and reduced the Taino natives to slavery. After fifty-years of Spanish rule the Taino natives, who numbered between 3,000,000 to 4,000,000 prior to the advent of the Spanish, were decimated through the hardship of their condition as slaves, organized massacres, and diseases they contracted from the Spaniards (James, 1986; Fick, 1990; Nicholls, 1979; Du Bois, 2004, 2012; Buck-Morss, 2009).

The genocide of the Taino natives on the island was one of the most brutal in recorded history. As a result, Bartholomew de Las Casas, a Spanish priest, protested against the massacre of the Indians and demanded the cessation of the injustices committed against them. He advocated for the importation of blacks from Africa to work in the mines and on the plantations as a means of ending Indian slavery on the island. Thus, in 1503, the first Africans landed on the island. These initial Africans were indentured servants from Spain. Eventually, by 1697 Africans and the French would subsequently displace the Spanish on the western side of the island of Hispaniola.

In 1625, the first French adventurers landed on the island of La Tortue (Tortuga Island) in the northern part of what is today the Republic of Haiti. Later, they began exploring and settling on the main land to eventually displace the Spanish from the western part of the island through warfare. Tired of their attack, and also because of the results of war in Europe, Spain signed with France the Treaty of Ryswick in 1697, ceding to the latter the western part of the island. The French renamed their possession Saint-Domingue. The French developed Saint-Domingue/Haiti into the richest colony in the world through an export-oriented agricultural (plantation) economy based on enslaved Africans imported from West and Central Africa. To build this wealth, France imported thousands of slaves from Africa who, under France's *Code Noir*, or black codes, were submitted to virtually the same abuses and mistreatments imposed on the Taino natives by the Spanish.

Subsequently, the importation of Africans in large numbers would change the demographics of Saint-Domingue/Haiti. Under French rule, Saint-Domingue's population, as previously mentioned, was divided into three main social groups or classes, the whites or "Blancs", the "Affranchis", a group composed of free blacks and mulattoes, and the great masses of imported African slaves who constituted 75 percent of the population. By 1789, the colony's population comprised between 400,000 and 500,000 Africans, compared to about 40,000 whites and 30,000 mulattoes and free blacks or Affranchis (Fick, 1990; Du Bois, 2012). A great number of mulattoes were the offsprings of the union between "Blancs" and African women who were raped by their slavemasters. In many instances, slavemasters married the women, adopted these children, and provided them with the necessities of life. These offsprings would in-turn inherit the wealth of their fathers. Thus, by the end of the 18th century, the mulattoes would own around 25 to 30 percent of the colony's plantations and wealth, while most of them went to France to get a higher education (Fick, 1990; Nicholls, 1979; Du Bois, 2004). Nonetheless, in spite of their wealth and Western interpellation and embourgeoisement via the Catholic Church and French education, the mulattoes, because of their color, were considered inferior to the blancs or whites by law and were discriminated against. For example, they could not enter certain professions, i.e., law, medicine, etc., wear European clothes, or sit among the whites in church. They were reduced to a land and slave-owning merchant class who exported indigo, coffee, and other cash crops (Fick, 1990; Du Bois, 2004).

As a result of these discriminatory practices under the *Code Noir* of the colony, conflict arose between the *Affranchis*, particularly the *gens de couleur*, and the whites throughout the 18th century with the former claiming civil and political equality with the latter who wanted to maintain the status quo. Simultaneously, the whites on the island were demanding from France the right to participate in the running of the colony. They wanted to make of Saint-Domingue a country that would be autonomous from France. Both groups would voice their grievances at the time of the French revolution in 1789, which proclaimed the principles of liberty, equality and fraternity (James, 1986; Dupuy, 1989; Fick, 1990; Nicholls, 1979; Du Bois, 2004, 2012). In many instances, the *gens de couleur* , through their French supporters in Paris, *Société des Amis des Noirs* , did so at the expense of the free blacks whom they looked down upon on account of their race.

For the most part, however, the enslaved Africans and maroon communities of Africans in the mountainsides were neither a part of the conflict between the *Affranchis* and the whites, nor this claim for liberty, equality, and fraternity proclaimed by them. The Africans of Saint-Domingue/Haiti, for the most part, came from three regions of Africa: The Congo, Dahomey/ Benin, and the Nago regions of the continent (James, 1986; Fick, 1990; Desmangles, 1992; Du Bois, 2004, 2012). Although from different tribes of Africa what united the Africans together were the Vodou worldview, its ideological apparatuses, Lakous, peristyles, etc., and modes of production, husbandry, subsistence agriculture, and *komes*.[2] Unlike the British and Spanish colonies where Africans were bred like animals upon their arrival to the Americas, the French did not breed their enslaved Africans. Instead, upon illness, disability, and or death, they simply imported more Africans to replace the labor supply in the colonies. In the mind of the White landowners, it was actually less expensive to import enslave Africans than to breed them. Be that as it may, given the importation policy of the French planters coupled with the relative isolation of the newly arrived Africans on the island from the whites and Affranchis, the Africans imported to Saint-Domingue by the French were able to maintain and reproduce their African Vodou ideology, ideological apparatuses, practical consciousnesses, and social relations of production without any discontinuity in spite of the orders of the *Code Noirs*, which they tirelessly fought against.

The enslaved Africans who were brought to the French colonies manifested their rejection of their condition through different forms of resistance. Enslaved Africans poisoned their masters; others committed infanticide to save their offsprings from the hellish conditions of slavery (Genovese, 1979; Fick, 1990; Karenga, 1993; Du Bois, 2004). The most successful and persistent form of slave protest was marronage. Marronage consisted of slaves running away from the plantation to hide in the mountains of the island or in its forests where they reconstituted their African ways of life (Genovese, 1979; Fick, 1990; Desmangles, 1992; Karenga, 1993). From their retreat, the maroons also conducted raids on the plantations and often would come out at night to poison or kill their masters. One of the most famous Haitian maroons was François Mackandal . Mackandal was an *oungan*, or Vodou priest, from Guinea. At night, he would attack plantations, burning them and killing their owners. During his six-year rebellion, he and his followers poisoned and killed as many as 6000 whites. In 1758, however, the French captured him and publicly executed him on the public square of Cap Francais, present-day Cap-Haitian (Fick, 1990; Desmangles, 1992).

REVOLUTIONARY HAITI

The French Revolution of 1789 in France was not the spark that lit the Haitian Revolution of 1791 as many theorists propose (James, 1986; Du Bois, 2004, 2012). As previously highlighted, the revolution began the minute the Africans arrived on the island. However, the interests of the Africans were not the same as the interests of the other economic racial groups on the island, which created some very strange alliances and movements. Within an emerging Protestant capitalist world-system, France enforced a system called the "exclusif" on Saint-Domingue/Haiti. Similar to the capitalist world-system in globalization under American hegemony, this "exclusive" system required that Saint-Domingue sell 100 percent of her agricultural and raw material exports to France, and purchase 100 percent of her manufactured imports from them as well. The French merchants and crown set the prices for both imports and exports, and the prices were extraordinarily favorable to France and in no way competitive with world markets. This "exclusive" system was virtually the same as the one which England had forced on its North American colonies. Like the North Americans, the white and landowning *Affranchis* Saint-Domingueans did not abide strictly by this system. A contraband trade grew with the British in Jamaica and North America, and after its successful revolution, the United States. The Americans wanted molasses from Saint- Domingue for their burgeoning rum distilleries, and Saint-Domingue imported huge quantities of low quality dried fish to feed to the slaves. The planters (both white and free people of color) chafed under the oppression of France's "exclusif." There was a growing independence movement, and in this movement the white planters were united with the free people of color. It was a curious alliance, since the whites continued to oppress the free people of color in their social life, but formed a coalition with them on the political and economic front (Fick, 1990; Du Bois, 2004). Conversely, the petit-blancs remained outside this coalition, primarily because they were unwilling to form any sort of alliance with any persons of color, free or not. The petit-blancs were avowed racists and were especially offended and threaten by the elevated economic status of most of the free people of color. It is important to note that this economic independence movement did not include the slaves in any way whatsoever, who were enslaved by both the *Affranchis* and whites. Those who were a party to the movement were avowed slave owners and their vision of a free Saint-Domingue was liked that of the United States, a slave owning nation.

As such, the Africans, such as Armand, Martial, Macaya, Sans Souci, and others on the island, fought against the whites, mulattoes, and free persons of color (Fick, 1990). The slave owners, both white and people of color, i.e., free blacks and mulattoes, feared the Africans and knew that the incredible concentration of enslaved Africans (the slaves outnumbered the free people 10-1) required exceptional control. The owners tried to keep slaves of the same tribes apart; they forbade any meetings of slaves; and they tied slaves rigorously to their own plantations under the *Code Noir*. The Africans rebelled against these conditions. The African slave rebellions were without allies among the whites, mulattoes, or free people of color. They were not even fully united among themselves, and the domestic slaves, like their American counterparts, especially tended to be more loyal to their masters than the field slaves. The maroons, in the meantime, were in contact with rebellious slaves, but they had few firm alliances. Nonetheless, their hatred of slavery, their fear of being re-enslaved, and their desire to be free and safe in their own country, made them ready allies were a serious slave revolution to begin. In the mountains they practiced their Vodou religions, reproduced its ideological apparatuses, and modes of production, i.e., subsistence agriculture, husbandry, and *komes* (Genovese, 1979; Fick, 1990; Du Bois, 2012).

So by 1790 one year before the official commencement of the Revolution, the colony was divided between French bureaucrats, white planters, petit-blancs, mulatto elites, free people of color, enslaved Africans, and maroons each with their own agendas, alliances, and worldviews or structuring structures (Genovese, 1979; Fick, 1990; Du Bois, 2004). The split between the two colonial white groups gave strength to the French government officials who had lost effective control of the colony. The mulatto elites despised the free persons of color based solely on race and class, while at the same time forming a strange alliance with the white elites, who in alliance with the petit-blancs discriminated against them. Meanwhile, the maroons distrusted all the groups including the enslaved (house and field) Africans who were left to their own devices on the plantations. Each of these forces was poised to strike against the other. Yet, in the crazy contradictions of this whole situation, the petit-blancs and white planters each carried on their own private war of terror against the mulattoes, free people of color, and the enslaved Africans. These divisions among maroon and enslaved Africans, slave owners, the divisions among the whites, free persons of color, and mulattoes, were not only racial and economic, they were sociocultural as well, European (an emerging Protestant Ethic and the spirit of capitalism) on the one hand, and African (The Vodou Ethic and the spirit of communism) on the other (Genovese, 1979). Many scholars (James, 1986; Dupuy, 1989; DuBois, 2012) overlook this sociocultural component or sweep it in the literature by referring to the Africans as masses, peasants, maroons, or blacks. As though, outside of the dominant European worldview, which the Affranchis internalized and sought to reproduce, the Africans had no other worldview to recursively reorganize or reproduce in the material world (Genovese, 1979).

DISCUSSION

Typically historians date the beginnings of the Haitian Revolution with the uprising of the slaves on the night of August 14th, 1791. On August 14th, 1791, as the whites and the Affranchis continued on their war for greater participation in the running of the colony and for equality of opportunity, recognition, and distribution, the African maroons entered into a full-fledge rebellion that would ultimately result in the creation of the nation-state of Haiti and the abolition of slavery on the island. Boukman Dutty , another oungan following the path of Mackandal, organized a meeting with the diverse African tribes of the island in the mountains of the Northern corridors of the island. This meeting, referred to as *minokan* in the Vodou tradition, took the form of a spiritual Petwo Vodou ceremony. According to Haitian folklore, it was raining and the sky was raging with clouds. The elders and representatives of the African tribes began the ceremony by confessing their resentment for their condition. A woman, Cecile Fatiman, a Vodou manbo priestess, started dancing languorously in the crowd, taken by the spirits of the lwa, African lunar Goddess, Erzulie Danthor. With a knife in her hand, she cut the throat of a black pig (according to Max Beauvoir, the current *ATI-oungan* of Vodou today, an actual person was sacrificed that night. Black pig, *Kochon noir*, refers to the nomenclature given to maroon Africans by the French.), a sacrifice to Danthor, and distributed the blood to all the participants of the meeting who swore to unite, kill all of the whites and mulattoes on the island with the aid of Manbo Danthor, and constitute a new equitable society based on the principles of Bon-dye. Manbo Fatima/Danthor proceeded to layout the leadership of the rebellion, naming Georges Biassou, Jeannot, Jean Francois, Macaya, etc. On August 22, 1791, the blacks of the North entered into a rebellion, killing all the whites and mulattoes they met and setting the plantations of the colony on fire.

The French quickly captured the leader of the slaves, Boukman , and beheaded him, bringing the rebellion under control. Just like Mackandal, however, Boukman had managed to instill in the blacks the idea of his invincibility. Thus, the French exposed his head on Cap's square to convince the slaves that their leader was really dead. The death of Boukman, although it had temporarily stopped the rebellion of the North, it failed, however, to restrain the rest of the blacks from revolting against their condition. Toussaint Louverture, a free literate black *Affranchis* , and Jean-Jacques Dessalines, an enslaved first generation Saint-Dominguean/Haitian (creole field slave) whose parents were directly from Africa, would assume the leadership of the revolt after the death of Boukman.

Unlike Boukman, who was a charismatic leader that incorporated the maroon West African slaves', sixty-seven percent of whom were directly from Africa when the Revolution commenced, Vodou spiritualism, and culture to organize the rebellion at Bois Caïman against the *blancs* and *Affranchis*, Toussaint Louverture, proved to be a military genius and a formidable leader in the tradition of the West. Toussaint, a literate free black who was treated well by his slavemaster and interpellated and embourgeoised by the church and his slavemaster, who taught him to read, did not exclude the *Affranchis* from the revolution. He organized the maroons, masses of slaves, and a few *Affranchis* free slaves and mulattoes into an organized army. With political manipulation, and military campaigns, he would gain notoriety in the colony. During the period of 1791 to 1800, Toussaint outmaneuvered the French, the Spaniards, and the English. He managed to eliminate all his enemies on the island until he was the only power left in Saint-Domingue/ Haiti. By 1801, he governed the entire island, and proclaimed himself governor-general of the colony. A constitution was soon drawn-up that same year declaring Saint-Domingue an autonomous French black possession where slavery was abolished.

Although Toussaint abolished slavery on the island, he maintained the exported-oriented agricultural system of slavery under a new share-cropping partnership between the Africans and their former slavemasters who became cultivators. Many of the maroons and mulatto elites (Andre Rigaud, Alexander Pétion, Jean-Pierre Boyer, etc.) rebelled against Toussaint's position and continued their fight against his army of free blacks, whites, and mulattoes. The former, maroon Africans, did so because they were against anything that resembled slavery, and the latter, mulatto elites, due to the emergence of the new free black property classes composed of the generals in Toussaint's army and the continuing economic role of the whites. Defeated in what is famously referred to as "the war of knives" by Jean-Jacques Dessalines, the mulattoes André Rigaud, Alexandre Pétion, and Jean-Pierre Boyer would leave for France, while Macaya, Sans Souci, and many of the African maroons either became landowners or returned to the mountains leaving Toussaint in control of the plantation system. Hence the pre-1791 status-quo was re-instituted under Toussaint without slavery.

Following his European campaign, Napoleon Bonaparte wary of Toussaint's great power in the colony sent 82,000 of his battle proven troops commanded by the mulattoes Alexandre Pétion, Jean-Pierre Boyer, and his brother-in-law, General Leclerc, a fleet of warships, canons, munitions and dogs in order to quell the rebellion and recapture Haiti as a slave colony. Whereas the *Affranchis* surrendered, the Africans under the leadership of Sans Souci and Macaya continued their warfare against the French and Affranchis from the mountains. Two years of war ended in a stalemate; however, the French treacherously arrested Toussaint Louverture during a meeting in June 1802. He was exiled to France and died in the *Fort de Joux* prison high in the cold Alpine mountains of Jura in April 1803.

With the arrest, and eventual death, of Toussaint, Jean-Jacques Dessalines, a trained oungan in the traditions of Macandal and Boukman, whose dislike for the whites and mulatto *Affranchis* was not shared by Louverture, formed a shaky alliance with the maroon Africans, free blacks, and mulattoes (under the leadership of Alexandre Pétion who was sent back under Leclerc's army to reclaim the island for France) and emerged as the new leader of the Haitian Revolution, bringing it, with the aid of Henri Christophe, Francois Capois-la-Mort, and the maroon Africans to its ultimate climax, the first black independent republic in the world on January 1, 1804. Unlike Toussaint, Dessalines was a field slave interpellated and ounganified/manboified by the Vodou ideology and ideological apparatuses of the Africans. He had no formal Western education and disagreed with Toussaint over the roles of the mulattoes and whites in the revolution. Nonetheless, in his eventual move to liberate Haiti, he united with the maroon Africans, free blacks, and mulatto elites led by Alexandre Pétion. Haiti's revolution against colonialism and slavery was the first successful black movement resulting in an independent state headed by so-called blacks. On January 1, 1804 Dessalines, to honor the Taino natives who had been massacred by the Spanish, renamed the island its original Tainoian name, Haiti or Ayi-ti (mountainous land). Since these glorious events, Haiti has been the pariah of the West bearing the mark of the poorest country in the Hemisphere. This distinction is a product of the racial-class divisions between the mulattoes, free blacks, and the Africans, which would continue in Haiti during and following the Revolution and the death of Jean-Jacques Dessalines.

Following the Revolution, Haiti was marginalized by all the European powers of the time, and fighting amongst the three remaining groups, the mulatto elites, the free black generals, and the African maroons, emerged over the constitution of the new nation-state. The mulatto elites desired the land of their white fathers, the free black generals wanted to maintain their land they had obtained from Toussaint during the early parts of the war, and the African maroons wanted no parts of anything that resembled the old system of slavery or Toussaint's *corvée* system. The former two, interpellated and embourgeoised by the ideology and ideological apparatuses of the West, sought to reproduce the same colonial system as their former colonial slavemasters, while the latter and the majority of the population interpellated and ounganified/manboified by the leadership of the Vodou Ethic and the spirit of communism did not. Instead, they went about practicing their religion, husbandry, subsistence agriculture, and komes as enframed by the Vodou Ethic and the spirit of communism. Dessalines sought to constitute the new nation-state within these two opposing structuring structures. As such in his 1805 constitution he proceeded to divide the land equitably among all those who fought in the Revolution; renounced everything that was French for systems grounded in the experiences of the people of the island; and renounced white supremacy for a pan-African discourse that would have Haiti become the land for and of blacks (Fick, 1990; Nicholls, 1979; Du Bois, 2012).

This constitution of Haiti did not sit well with the *Affranchis* who desired their pre-war status and wealth. Instead of focusing on fortification of the island, national production, food security, and agricultural production for local consumption as Dessalines attempted to do with his equitable redistribution of land among the population, the *Affranchis* assassinated him over his land reform and the masses of Africans fled to the mountainsides. With the death of Dessalines, the majority of the productive land was divided among the mulatto elites, who took over their fathers' land and estates, and the black commanding officers of the revolution. They kept intact the export based economic arrangements which existed under colonialism and Toussaint's regime with the mulatto elites—because of their status as mulattoes—serving as the middle persons between the nation-state and outside merchants. What emerged in Haiti, following the Revolution, was the same colonial class structure under the leadership of the Affranchis and their adversarial partnership with an emerging foreign white merchant class, which assisted in the acquisition of manufactured goods, petit-bourgeois blacks who converted their plantations into agribusinesses, and the Africans in the provinces and mountains whose products were heavily taxed by the emerging nation-state under the leadership of the Affranchis (Pierre-Louis, 2000; Du

Bois, 2012). As Francois Pierre-Louis (2000) brilliantly highlights of the emerging Haitian racial-class structure following the Revolution,

> The ostracism of Haiti by the major powers also affected inter-class relationships. In order to obtain cash, the revolutionary governments kept intact the export based economic arrangements which existed under colonialism. The most productive lands in the country were divided between the generals and their families for the cultivation of cash crops. Most of the slaves who fought in the independence war had to resign themselves to working small parcels of land in the mountains for their subsistence. As a result of this arrangement, the class structure of Haiti evolved into three categories: The vast landowners (made up primarily of generals and relatives of the fleeing colonists who moved up the ranks under revolutionary governments), the merchant class and the landless peasants. The large landowners encouraged the production of cash crops on their plantation through a system of share cropping. . . Soon after the revolution the government attempted to restore a forced labor system called *corvée* on the plantations in order to restore Haiti's pre-independence level of productivity in commodities such as coffee and sugar. The leaders had a tough time enforcing the forced labor system due to massive resistance from the former slaves. Instead, a system of share cropping was instituted through which they succeeded in obtaining a substantial labor from the peasant population.
>
> After the large landowners came the merchant class. This class was composed primarily of descendants of the colonists and foreigners. The merchant class acted as an intermediary between the landowners and the external market. A symbiotic relationship developed between the landowning-class and the merchant class. This symbiotic relationship manifested itself in the property relations, the labor relations, and the mechanism of distribution that they both depended on to maintain their economic status. The only way the landowners could obtain manufactured goods was through the merchant class who in turn would sell Haiti's commodities in the international market. The primary role of the merchant class...was to sell the cash crops in the international market and buy manufactured goods for the local economy. Therefore, the landowning class depended on the merchant class for its manufactured goods while, the merchant class could not survive without the landowning class. Even though in some cases there were a few members of the merchant class who had large tracts of land, their main activities were in the import-export sector (pp. 6-7).

HAITI SINCE 1804

I do not completely share in the urban-rural and peasant-landowner-merchant dichotomy of Pierre-louis. Such a Marxian position negates the agential initiatives of the Africans, who, as I have demonstrated throughout this work, had a different structuring structure (form of system and social integration) from the mulatto elites and petit-bourgeois black landowners looking to the West, for equality of opportunity, recognition, and distribution. My phenomenological structural position is more Weberian than Marxian, and can be summed up as such. The impending defeat of the French in Haiti is widely credited with contributing to Napoleon's decision to sell the Louisiana territory to the United States in 1803. Haiti is the world's oldest black republic and the second-oldest republic in the Western Hemisphere after the United States. Although Haiti actively assisted the independence movements of many Latin American countries, the independent nation of former slaves was excluded from the hemisphere's first regional meeting of independent nations in Panama in 1826, and did not receive U.S. diplomatic recognition until 1862. In 1825, French officials arrived and informed the Haitian government that they were willing to recognize the country as a sovereign nation but it would do so on account that they pay compensation and reparation in exchange for the revolution. Whereas Dessalines and Henri Christophe rebuked this idea, the Haitians, following the death of Christophe, under the leadership of the Affranchis mulattoes, Alexandre Pétion and Jean-Pierre Boyer, seeking equality of opportunity, recognition, and distribution with their white counterparts in France agreed. The French government sent a team of accountants and actuaries into Haiti in order to place a value on all lands, all physical assets, the 500,000 citizens who were formerly enslaved (including members of the Cabinet who were also valued because they had been enslaved people before independence), animals, and all other commercial properties and services. The sums amounted to 150 million gold francs. Haiti was requested to pay this reparation to France in return for national recognition. The Haitian government under Boyer's administration agreed; payments began immediately. Boyer shut down all of the Western ideological apparatuses, schools, etc., in the provinces so that the masses could return to the *corvée* system in order to pay the independence debt, and went after Vodou through his anti-superstition laws (Ramsey, 2014; Du Bois, 2012).

Thus began the systematic destruction of the Republic of Haiti, and its dependent development within the capitalist world-system at the expense of the Africans in the provinces and mountains (Pierre-Louis, 2000; Nicholls, 1979; Du Bois, 2012). The French government bled the nation and rendered it a failed state. It was a merciless exploitation that was designed and guaranteed to collapse the Haitian economy and society. Haiti was forced, on the backs of the Africans in the provinces and mountains whose crops, they used for *komes*, were taxed heavily, to pay this sum until 1947 when the last installment was made. During the long 19th century, the payment to France amounted to up to 70 percent of the country's foreign exchange earnings. In the years when the coffee crops failed, or the sugar yield was down, the Haitian government borrowed on the French money market at double the going interest rate in order to repay the French government. When the Americans invaded the country in the early 20th century, 1915-1934, one of the reasons offered was to assist the French in collecting its reparations (Du Bois, 2012).

The collapse of the Haitian nation-state resides at the hands of France and America, especially, in alliance with the mulatto merchant and petit-bourgeois black landowning classes of the island serving as a Francophile neocolonial oligarchy seeking equality of opportunity, recognition, and distribution with whites against the African leadership of oungan yo, manbo yo, gangan yo, granmoun yo and the masses who sought to establish an independent nation-state for all blacks as envisioned by Dessalines.

What France did openly in the nineteenth and early twentieth-centuries, the United States, with the assistance of the landowning and merchant classes, continued clandestinely up to the twenty-first century.[3] After the revolution, two separate regimes—north and south—emerged, but were unified in 1820 under Boyer's government. Two years later, Haiti occupied Santo Domingo, the eastern, Spanish-speaking part of Hispaniola. In 1844, however, Santo Domingo, with the assistance of the Americans and the Spanish, broke away from Haiti and became the Dominican Republic. With 22 changes of government from 1843 to 1915, Haiti experienced numerous periods of intense political and economic disorder between the mulatto merchant and petit-bourgeois black landowning classes over control of the state apparatus, prompting, as previously mentioned, the United States' military intervention of 1915. It is under this occupation and America's southern brand of racism that the mulatto elites began to recognize their own racism towards the so-called black masses (Du Bois, 2012). Following the 19-year occupation, U.S. military forces were withdrawn in 1934, and Haiti regained sovereign rule under the leadership of the mulatto and merchant classes until 1957 when Francois "papa-doc" Duvalier assumed the presidency, declared himself president for life, and through his *noirisme* philosophy attempted to make the black landowning class the power elites of the society, undergirded by the *Tonton Macoutes* composed of members of the peasant class, against the mulatto elites and merchant classes. Duvalier, a former doctor in the provinces and mountains, also utilized elements from Vodou to buttress his power. As Francois Pierre-Louis further notes of this transition,

> The U.S. occupation restructured three major aspects of Haitian society: the army, public administration and class relationships. . . The marines refashioned the army making it the sole authority in the country and they gave it additional roles previously filled by civilians. The army called Gendarmerie built roads, supervised travel, collected census information, enforced various health and sanitation codes, and also supervised the prisons. . . By recruiting primarily light skinned Haitians, the marines further exacerbated the skin color conflict in the country. Even though the previous army was repressive, this was the first time a professional army in the country was created not to fight foreign enemies, but to oppress its own people. The new army created by the

Americans did not only fight Haitian peasants, but it repressed urbanites, students, and all others who dared challenge the occupiers. . . Another major aspect in the restructuring of the army was centralization. Whereas under the national army there were different points of power, the marines centralized the command center of the army. Port-au-Prince once again became the center of power. . . [Moreover, i]nstead of restructuring class relationship in Haiti as it has done elsewhere such as the Dominican Republic and several countries in Central America through massive investments in the agricultural sector, the United States practically left class relationships as it had found it. They made no land reforms or major attempts to integrate the peasant population into mainstream life. There were some investments in light manufacturing and processing plants, however, the bulk of the reform was in public administration. This reform eventually favored the merchant class as it had the technical and intellectual capacity to work in the reformed administration. Furthermore, the marines' racial prejudice exacerbated the color problem in the country. . . From 1915 to 1947, all the Haitian Presidents were mulattoes. . . From 1934 until the reign of Francois Duvalier, the army was the power broker in Haiti. No one was elected to rule the country without its prior approval. Whenever it did not like a President, it overthrew him. Francois Duvalier, who came to power with the acquiescence of the army, attempted to control it by introducing an alternative force called the Tonton Macoutes. The Tonton Macoutes were primarily peasants who were drafted as militia members by Duvalier to check the power of the Army. Using the *noiriste* propaganda, which advocated that black skinned Haitians should rule Haiti, Duvalier succeeded in allying a major sector of the middle class and large landowners to support him. To prevent the merchant class from using the army to stage a coup against him, he removed a number of mulatto generals in the military. He then replaced these generals with military personnel who supported his *noiriste* policies. Several attempts by the merchant class and its sympathizers in the military to overthrow Duvalier ended in catastrophe (2000, pgs., 7-9).

From February 7, 1986—when the 29-year dictatorship of the Duvalier family, backed by the CIA, ended—until 1991, Haiti was ruled by a series of provisional military governments trained and supported by the United States. In March 1987, with the fall of Duvalier, a constitution was ratified that provided for an elected, bicameral parliament; an elected president that served as head of state; and a prime minister, cabinet, ministers, and supreme court appointed by the president with parliament's consent. The Haitian Constitution (1987) also provides for political decentralization through the election of mayors and administrative bodies responsible for local government. Essentially, under the guise of the United States the attempt was to convert Haiti into an export-oriented Western neoliberal democratic capitalist state under the guise of what Robert Dahl refers to as a polyarchy, a democracy of rotating elites, the mulatto merchant/professional class and so-called black landowning professional and managerial class as their interests stood against the mode of production (subsistence agriculture, husbandry, and komes) and ideological apparatuses (Lakous, peristyles, etc.) of the Africans of the provinces and mountains.

In December 1990, in spite of US efforts to get Marc Bazin elected in an effort to facilitate their neoliberal agenda, the Haitian masses in Haiti's first democratic elections elected father Jean-Bertrand Aristide, a former Catholic priest, who won 67 percent of the vote in a presidential election that international observers deemed largely free and fair. Aristide took office on February 7, 1991, but was overthrown that September in a violent coup led by army elements supported by many of the country's economic elite, who were against Aristide's increase of the Haitian minimum wage and land and social policies for the peasant class who constituted over 65 percent of the population. The coup, given the political persecution that ensued, contributed to a large-scale exodus of Haitian peasants by boat to the United States. From October 1991 to September 1994 a de facto military regime governed Haiti. Various OAS and UN initiatives to end the political crisis through the peaceful restoration of the constitutionally elected government failed. On July 31, 1994, the UN Security Council adopted Resolution 940, which authorized member states to use all necessary means to facilitate the departure of Haiti's military leadership and to restore Haiti's constitutionally elected government to power. The United States took the lead in forming a multinational force (MNF) to carry out the UN's mandate by means of a military intervention. In mid-September, with U.S. troops prepared to enter Haiti by force, Gen. Raoul Cedras, a mulatto, and other top leaders agreed to accept the intervention of the MNF. On September 19, 1994, the first contingents of what became a 21,000-member international force touched down in Haiti to oversee the end of military rule and the restoration of the constitutional government. President Aristide and other elected officials exiled in the US returned on October 15. Upon his return, Aristide disbanded the army, and served out the remainder of his five-year term. As the Haitian constitution of 1987 prevents back to back terms, Aristide was replaced by his former prime-minister Rene Préval in 1995. Following Préval's, a former Marxist, first term Aristide was reelected in 2000. Once again, however, Aristide, in a coup led by the merchant class, mulatto elites, and petit-bourgeois classes, the United States, Canada, and France, who were against his liberation theology, leftist-leaning economic policies, Africanization of Haiti via his attempt to make Vodou and Kreyol the national religion and language of the island, and suit in the World Court to obtain the 150 million francs, with interest, from France, which Haiti had to pay following the Revolution, was eventually deposed in February 2004 and sent into Exile to South Africa. Following the brief stance of a provisional government, Aristide was subsequently replaced by Rene Préval who was governing the nation when the massive earthquake of January 12, 2010 that killed almost 200,000 to 230,000 citizens struck the island. Préval was subsequently replaced by Michel Martelly, a mulatto and former Konpas singer, who the US backed in flawed elections to implement their and the economic classes' neoliberal agenda, which they had started under Jean-Claude Duvalier, under the slogan, "Haiti is Open for Business." Under this mantra the emphasis is on high-end tourism for the economic elites of the Protestant capitalist world-system, export-oriented agro-industry, athletics (soccer and basketball), and textile and manufacturing sweatshops.

CONCLUSIONS

At the time of the writing of this work, Haiti, under a United Nations force (MINUSTAH), continues to be under occupation within the capitalist world-system under American hegemony. The continuous struggle between the mulatto merchant/professional class and the black landowning managerial classes for control of the state and its apparatuses, at the expense of the African masses in the provinces and mountains whose children they arm and use against each other as they migrate to Port-au-Prince amidst American neoliberal policies seeking to displace the masses for tourism, agro and textile industries, and athletics (basketball and soccer) continues to be a hindrance for the constitution of a sovereign Haitian nation-state. The former two, interpellated and embourgeoised in Western ideological apparatuses, seek to constitute Haiti, with the aid of whites (France, Canada, and America), as an export-oriented periphery state within the capitalist world-system under American hegemony against the desires of the masses of Africans in the provinces and mountains seeking to maintain their *komes*, subsistence agriculture, and husbandry, which are deemed informal. Instead of focusing on infrastructure (artificial lakes, potable water, food security, mache—modern market spaces for *komes*, universities, etc.) to augment national agriculture and the productive forces of the latter group, who constitute eighty-five percent of the population, the mulatto elites and petit-bourgeois blacks emphasize job creation through foreign direct investment in tourism, agro and textile industries, privatization of public services, and infrastructure for an export-oriented economy similar to the one they had under slavery. However, their inabilities—given the voting power of the majority—to constitute two dominant rotating political parties to implement the desires of their former colonial slavemasters, leaves Haiti in perpetual turmoil. As in slavery, the African masses continue to fight, against their interpellation, embourgeoisement, and differentiation as wage-earners in the tourism trade and textile factories of the Catholic/Protestant Ethic and spirit of capitalism of these two power elites seeking equality of opportunity, recognition, and distribution with whites at their expense, for the Vodou Ethic and the spirit of communism of *oungan yo, manbo yo,* and *granmoun yo* of Bois Caiman and Jean-

Jacques Dessalines. As the current historical conjuncture parallels the conjuncture of 1791 either a unifying national conference that parallels Bois Caiman or a second war of independence will determine the outcome of this perpetual economic and cultural civil war in Haiti.

NOTES

1. The term marronage fails to capture the practical consciousness by which the Africans of Haiti went about recursively reorganizing and reproducing their world. Eugene Genovese, in his usage of the term, is one scholar who does.

2. By emphasizing Vodou over Islam, which also united many of the Africans from the Congo region, the intent is not to minimize it. Instead, my intent is to highlight the fact that in spite of the fact that many Africans adopted Islam they still held on to their original tribal faiths, which united them in the colonies.

3. The Americans would be responsible for the centralization of all economic activities in the capital city, Port-au-Prince. Prior to their occupation, the country was decentralized under the ruling of different generals.

References Cited

Adorno, Theodor W. (2000). *Negative Dialectics*. New York: Continuum.

Allen, Ernest Jr. (2002). "Du Boisian Double Consciousness: The Unsustainable Argument." *The Massachusetts Review*, 43 (2): 217–253.

Allen, Ernest Jr. (1992). "Ever Feeling One's Twoness: 'Double Ideals and 'Double Consciousness' in the Souls of Black Folk." *Critique of Anthropology*, 12 (3): 261–275.

Allen, Richard L. (2001). *The Concept of Self: A Study of Black Identity and Self Esteem*. Detroit: Wayne State University Press.

Alleyne, M. (1980). *Comparative Afro-American*. Ann Arbor: Karoman Press. (1989) *The Roots of Jamaican Culture* . London: Pluto Press.

Althusser, Louis (2001). *Lenin and Philosophy and Other Essays*. New York: Monthly Review Press.

Althusser, Louis and Étienne Balibar (1970). *Reading Capital* (Ben Brewster, Trans.). London: NLB.

Altschuler, Richard (ed.) (1998). *The living Legacy of Marx, Durkheim, and Weber: Applications and Analyses of Classical Sociological Theory by Modern Social Scientists*. New York: Gordian Knot Books.

Appiah, Anthony (1985). "The Uncompleted Argument: Du Bois and the Illusion of Race." *Critical Inquiry*, 12: 21–37.

Aptheker, Herbert (ed.) (1985). *W.E.B. Du Bois Against Racism: Unpublished Essays, Papers, Addresses, 1887–1961*. Amherst: The University of Massachusetts Press.

Archer, Kevin et al (2007). "Locating Globalizations and Cultures." *Globalizations*, 4, 1: 1–14.

Archer, L. (2009) The 'Black' Middle classes and Education: Parents and Young. People's Constructions of Identity, Values and Educational Practices. Paper Presented to British Education Research Association (BERA) September. University of Manchester.

Archer, L. (2011) Constructing Minority Ethnic Middle-class identity: An Exploratory Study with Parents, Pupils and Young Professionals. *Sociology* 45 (1): 134–151.

Archer, L. & Francis, B. (2007) *Understanding Minority Ethnic Achievement: Race, Gender, Class and 'Success'*. London: Routledge.

Archer, Margaret S. (1985). "Structuration versus Morphogenesis." In H.J. Helle and S.N. Eisenstadt (Eds.), *Macro-Sociological Theory: Perspectives on Sociological Theory* (Volume 1) (pp. 58–88). United Kingdom: J.W. Arrowsmith Ltd.

Asante, Molefi Kete (1988). *Afrocentricity*. New Jersey: Africa World.

Asante, Molefi K. (1990a). *Kemet, Afrocentricity and Knowledge*. New Jersey: Africa World.

Austin, J.L. (1997). *How to do Things With Words* (Second edition, J.O. Urmson and Marina Sbisà, editors). Cambridge, Massachusetts: Harvard University Press.

Bailey, B.L. (1966). *Jamaican Creole Syntax*. Cambridge: Cambridge University Press.

Baker, Houston A., Jr. (1985). "The Black Man of Culture: W.E.B. Du Bois and The Souls of Black Folk." In William L. Andrews (Ed.), *Critical Essays on W.E.B. Du Bois* (pp.129–139). Boston: G.K. Hall & Co.

Balibar, Etienne & Immanuel Wallerstein (1991 [1988]). *Race, Nation, Class: Ambiguous Identities*. London: Verso.

Ballantine, Jeanne, H. (1993). *The Sociology of Education: A systematic Analysis* (3rd Edition). New Jersey: Prentice Hall.

Barone, C. (2006). Cultural Capital, Ambition and the Explanation of Inequalities in Learning Outcomes: A Comparative Analysis. *Sociology*, 40 (6): 1039–1058.

Barrs, M. and Cork, V. (2001). *The Reader in the Writer: The Links between the Study of Literature and Writing Development at Key Stage 2*. London: Centre for Language in Primary Education.

Barthes, Roland (1972). *Mythologies* (Annette Lavers, Trans.). New York: Hill and Wang.

Bashi, V and Hughes, M. (1997). Globalization and Residential Segregation by 'Race.' *Annuls of the American Academy of Social and Political Science*, 551: 105–20.

Beauvoir, Max (2006). "Herbs and Energy: The Holistic Medical System of the Haitian People." In Bellegarde-Smith, Patrick and Claudine Michel (eds.) *Haitian Vodou: Spirit, Myth, & Reality* (pgs. 112–133). Bloomington, IN: Indiana University Press.

Bellegarde-Smith, Patrick and Claudine Michel (2006). *Haitian Vodou: Spirit, Myth, &Reality*. Bloomington, IN: Indiana University Press.

Bell, Daniel (1985). *The Social Sciences Since the Second World War*. New Brunswick (USA): Transaction Books.

Bell, Bernard W. et al (editors) (1996). *W. E. B. Du Bois on Race and Culture: Philosophy, Politics, and Poetics*. New York and London: Routledge.

Bell, Bernard W. (1996). "Genealogical Shifts in Du Bois's Discourse on Double Consciousness as the Sign of African American Difference." In Bernard W. Bell et al (Eds.), *W.E.B. Du Bois on Race and Culture: Philosophy, Politics, and Poetics* (pp. 87–108). New York and London: Routledge.

Bell, Bernard W. (1985). "W.E.B. Du Bois's Struggle to Reconcile Folk and High Art." In William L. Andrews (Ed.), *Critical Essays on W.E.B. Du Bois* (pp.106–122). Andrews. Boston: G.K. Hall & Co.

Bennett, Lerone (1982). *Before the Mayflower*. Chicago: Johnson Publishing Company .

Bernstein, B. (1971*) Class, Codes and Control*. New York: Schocken Books.

Berthoud, R. (2000) Ethnic Employment Penalties in Britain. *Journal of Ethnic and Migration Studies*. 26 (3): pp. 389–416.

Bhabha, Homi (1995a). "Cultural Diversity and Cultural Differences." In Bill Ashcroft et al (Eds.), *The Post-colonial Studies Reader* (pp. 206–209). London and New York: Routledge.

Bhabha, Homi (1995b). "Signs Taken for Wonders." In Bill Ashcroft et al (Eds.), *The Post-colonial Studies Reader* (pp. 29–35). London and New York: Routledge.

Bhabha, Homi (1994). "Remembering Fanon: Self, Psyche and the Colonial Condition." In Patrick Williams and Laura Chrisman (Eds.), *Colonial Discourse and Post-Colonial Theory A Reader* (pp. 112–123). New York: Columbia University Press.

Bickerton, D. (1975). *Dynamics of a Creole System*. Cambridge: Cambridge University Press.

Billingsley, Andrew (1968). *Black Families in White America*. New Jersey: Prentice Hall.

Billingsley, Andrew (1970). "Black Families and White Social Science." *Journal of Social Issues*, 26, 127–142.

Billingsley, Andrew (1993). *Climbing Jacob's Ladder: The Enduring Legacy of African American Families*. New York: Simon & Schuster.

Bizzell, Patricia and Bruce Herzberg (2001). *The Rhetorical Tradition: Readings from Classical Times to the Present*. Boston: Bedford/St. Martin's.

Blackaby, D.H, Leslie, D.G.& Murphy, :D. (2005) N. C. O'Leary Born in Britain: How Are Native Ethnic Minorities faring in the British Labor Market? *Economic Letters* 88 (3): 370–375.

Blassingame, John W. (1972). *The Slave Community: Plantation Life in the Antebellum South*. New York: Oxford University Press.

Bleich, E. (2003) *Race and Politics in Britain and France: Ideas and Policy-making since the 1960s*. Cambridge: Cambridge University Press.

Boskin, Joseph (1965). "Race Relations in Seventeenth-Century America: The Problem of the Origins of Negro Slavery." In Donald Noel (Ed.), *The Origins of American Slavery and Racism* (pp. 95–105). Ohio: Charles E. Merrill Publishing Co.

Boswell, Terry (1989). "Colonial Empires and the Capitalist World-Economy: A Time Series Analysis of Colonization, 1640–1960." *American Sociological Review*, 54, 180–196.

Bourdieu, Pierre (1984). *Distinction: A Social Critique of the Judgement of Taste* (Richard Nice, Trans.). Cambridge MA: Harvard University Press.

Bourdieu, P. (1986). The Forms of Capital. In J.E. Richardson (Ed.), *Handbook of Theory and Research for the Sociology of Education* (pp. 241–258). Westport: Greenwood Press.

Bourdieu, Pierre (1990). *The Logic of Practice* (Richard Nice, Trans.). Stanford, California: Stanford University Press.

Boxill, Bernard R. (1996). "Du Bois on Cultural Pluralism." In Bell W. Bernard et al (Eds.), *W.E.B. Du Bois on Race and Culture: Philosophy, Politics, and Poetics* (pp. 57–86). New York and London: Routledge.

Brathwaite, E. (1984). *History of the Voice*. London: New Beacon Books.

Brecher, Jeremy and Tim Costello (1998). *Global Village or Global Pillage: Economic Reconstruction from the bottom up* (second ed.). Cambridge, Mass.: South End Press.

Brennan, Teresa (1997). "The Two Forms of Consciousness." *Theory Culture & Society*, 14 (4): 89–96.

Broderick, Francis L. (1959). *W.E.B. Du Bois, Negro Leader in a Time of Crisis*. Stanford, California: Stanford University Press.

Brown, C. (1985) *Black and White Britain*. London: Policy Studies Institute.

Bruce, Dickinson D., Jr. (1992). "W.E.B. Du Bois and the Idea of Double Consciousness." *American Literature*, 64: 299–309.

Bryne, D. (2001) *Understanding the Urban*. London: Palgrave.

Buck-Morss, Susan (2009). *Hegel, Haiti, and Universal History*. Pittsburgh: University of Pittsburgh Press.

Bullock Report (1975). *A Language for Life*. London. HMSO.

Byron, M. (1994) Post-war Caribbean Migration to Britain. The Unfinished Cycle. Aldershot: Avebury.

Carrington, L.D. (2001). The status of Creole in the Caribbean. In P. Christie (Ed.), *Due Respect: Papers on English and English-Related Creoles in the Caribbean in Honor of Professor Robert Le Page* (pp. 24–36). Mona, Kingston: University of the West Indies Press.

Caws, Peter (1997). *Structuralism: A Philosophy for the Human Sciences*. New York: Humanity Books.

Chanda-Goo, S. (2006) *South Asian Communities; Catalysts for Educational Change*. Stoke-on-Trent: Trentham.

Chase-Dunn, Christopher and Peter Grimes (1995). "World-Systems Analysis." *Annual Review of Sociology*, 21, 387–417.

Chase-Dunn, Christopher and Richard Rubinson (1977). "Toward a Structural Perspective on the World-System." *Politics & Society*, 7: 4, 453–476.

Chase-Dunn, Christopher (1975). "The effects of international economic dependence on development and inequality: A cross-national study." *American Sociological Review*, 40, 720–738.

Chiswick, B. (1978) The effect of Americanization on the Earnings of Foreign Born Men. *Journal of Political Economy*, 86 (5), pp.897–922.

Christie, P. (2003). *Language in Jamaica*. Kingston, Jamaica: Arawak.

Clark, K and Drinkwater, S. (2007) *Ethnic Minorities in the Labor Market: Dynamics and Diversity*. Abingdon: Joseph Rowntree Foundation. Policy Press.

Clark, Robert P. (1997). *The Global Imperative: An Interpretive History of the Spread of Humankind*. Boulder, Colorado: Westview Press.

Clarke, John Henrik, et. al. (eds.) (1970). *Black Titan: W.E.B. Du Bois*. Boston: Beacon Press.

Clark, P. (1988) *Prejudice and Your Child*. Middletown, Connecticut: Wesleyan University Press.

Coard, B. (1971) *How the Education West Indian Child is Made Educationally Subnormal in the British School System: The Scandal of the Black Child in School*. London: New Beacon Books.

Cohen, J. (2002). *Protestantism and Capitalism: The Mechanisms of Influence*. New York: Aldine de Gruyter.

Cole, M. (2011) Racism and Education in the UK and US. Palgrave Macmillan. New York.

Collinson, Diane (1987). *Fifty Major Philosophers: A Reference Guide*. London: Routledge.

Coser, Lewis (1956). *The functions of social conflict*. New York: The Free Press.

Covino, William A. and David A. Jolliffe (1995). *Rhetoric: concepts, definitions, boundaries*. Needham Heights, Massachusetts: Allyn and Bacon.

Cox, C.B. and Boyson, R. (1977) *Black Paper 1977*. London: Temple-Smith.

Craig, D.R. (1976). Bidialectal education: Creole and Standard in the West Indies. *IJSL* 8: 93–134.

Crosley, Reginald O. (2006). "Shadow-Matter Universes in Haitian and Dagara Ontologies: A Comparative Study." In Bellegarde-Smith, Patrick and Claudine Michel (eds.) *Haitian Vodou: Spirit, Myth, & Reality* (pgs. 7–18). Bloomington, IN: Indiana University Press.

Crothers, Charles (2003). "Technical Advances in General Sociological Theory: The Potential Contribution of Post-Structurationist Sociology." *Perspectives*, 26: (3), 3–6.

Crouch, Stanley (1993). "Who are We? Where Did We Come From? Where Are We Going?" In Gerald Early (Ed.), *Lure and Loathing: Essays on Race, Identity, and the Ambivalence of Assimilation* (pp. 80–94). New York: The Penguin Press.

Culler, Jonathan (1976). *Saussure*. Great Britain: Fontana/Collins.

Curtin, Philip D. (1969). *The Atlantic Slave Trade: A Census*. Madison, Wisconsin: The University of Wisconsin Press.

Dahrendorf, Ralf (1959). *Class and Class Conflict in Industrial Society*. Stanford, California: Stanford University Press.

Dayan, Joan (1998). Haiti, History, and the Gods. Berkeley and Los Angeles: University of California Press.

Degler, Carl N. (1972). "Slavery and the Genesis of American Race Prejudice." In Donald Noel (Ed.), *The Origins of American Slavery and Racism* (pp. 59–80). Ohio: Charles E. Merrill Publishing Co.

DeMarco, Joseph P. (1983). *The Social Thought of W.E.B. Du Bois*. Lanham, MD: University Press of America.

Deren, Maya (1972). *The Divine Horsemen: The Voodoo Gods of Haiti*. New York: Delta Publishing Co.

Desmangles, Leslie G. (1992). *The Faces of the Gods: Vodou and Roman Catholicism in Haiti*. Chapel Hill: The University of North Carolina Press.

Devonish, H. (1986). *Language and Liberation: Creole Language Politics in the Caribbean*. London: Karia Press.

Diop, Cheikh A. (1981). *Civilization or Barbarism: An Authentic Anthropology*. New York: Lawrence Hill Books.

Diop, Cheikh A. (1988). *Precolonial Black Africa*. Chicago: Chicago Review Press.

Diop, Cheikh A. (1989). *The African Origin of Civilization: Myth or Reality*. Chicago: Chicago Review Press.

Dogson, E. (1986) *Motherland: West Indian Women to Britain in the 1950s*. London: Heinemann Education Books.

Douglas, M. (1986). *How Institutions Think*. New York: Syracuse University Press.

Drake, St. Claire (1965). "The Social and Economic Status of the Negro in the United States." In Talcott Parsons and Kenneth B. Clark (Eds.), *The Negro American* (pp. 3–46). Boston: Houghton Mifflin Company.

Du Bois, Laurent (2004). *Avengers of the New World: The Story of the Haitian Revolution*. Cambridge, Massachusetts: Harvard University Press.

Du Bois, Laurent (2012). Haiti: The Afterschocks of History. New York: Metropolitan Books.

Du Bois, W.E.B. (1995 [1903]). *The Souls of Black Folk*. New York: Penguin Putnam Inc.

Du Bois, W.E.B. (1984 [1940]). *Dusk of Dawn: An Essay toward an Autobiography of a Race Concept*. New Brunswick and London: Transaction Books.

Du Bois, W.E.B. (1971a [1897]). "The Conservation of Races." In Julius Lester (Ed.), *The Seventh Son: The Thought and Writings of W.E.B. Du Bois* (Volume I) (pp. 176–187). New York: Random House.

Du Bois, W.E.B. (1971b [1935]). "A Negro Nation Within The Nation." In Julius Lester (Ed.), *The Seventh Son: The Thought and Writings of W.E.B. Du Bois* (Volume II) (pp. 399–407). New York: Random House.

Du Bois, W.E.B. (1970 [1939]). *Black Folk, Then and Now: An Essay in the History and Sociology of the Negro Race*. New York: Octagon Books.

Du Bois, W. E. B. (1968). *The Autobiography of W.E.B. Du Bois: A Soliloquy on Viewing My Life from the Last Decade of its First Century*. US: International Publishers Co., Inc.

Du Bois, W.E.B. (1967 [1899]). *The Philadelphia Negro: A Social Study*. New York: Schocken Books.

Dupuy, Alex (1989). *Haiti in the World Economy: Class, Race, and Underdevelopment Since 1700*. Boulder, CO: Westview Press.

Durkheim, Emile (1984 [1893]). *The Division of Labor in Society* (W.D. Halls, Trans.). New York: The Free Press.

Eagleton, Terry (1999). *Marx*. New York: Routledge.

Eagleton, Terry (1991). *Ideology: An Introduction*. London: Verso.

Early, Gerald (ed.) (1993). *Lure and Loathing: Essays on Race, Identity , and the Ambivalence of Assimilation*. New York: The Penguin Books.

Edgar, Andrew and Peter Sedgwick (Eds.) (1999). *Key Concepts in Cultural Theory*. London: Routledge.

Economic and Social Survey (2001). Jamaica: Planning Institute of Jamaica.

Elkins, Stanley (1959). *Slavery: A Problem in American Institutional and Intellectual Life*. Chicago: University of Chicago Press.

Elkins, Stanley M. (1972). "The Dynamics of Unopposed Capitalism." In Donald Noel (Ed.), *The Origins of American Slavery and Racism* (pp. 45–58). Ohio: Charles E. Merrill Publishing Co.

Engels, Frederick (2000 [1884]. *The Origin of the Family, Private Property, and the State*. New York: Pathfinder Press.

Fanon, Frantz (1967). *Black Skin, White Masks* (Charles Lam Markmann, Trans.). New York: Grove Press.

Fanon, Frantz (1963). *The Wretched of the Earth* (Constance Farrington, Trans). New York: Grove Press.

Fick, Carolyn E. (1990). *The Making of Haiti: The Saint Domingue Revolution from Below*. Knoxville, Tennessee: The University of Tennessee Press.

Fleurant, Gerdés (2006). "Vodun, Music, and Society in Haiti: Affirmation and Identity." In Bellegarde-Smith, Patrick and Claudine Michel (eds.) *Haitian Vodou: Spirit, Myth, & Reality* (pgs. 45–57). Bloomington, IN: Indiana University Press.

Fogel, Robert W. (2003). *The Slavery Debates, 1952–1990: A Retrospective*. Baton Rouge: Louisiana State University Press.

Foner, Eric (1988). *Reconstruction: America's Unfinished Revolution 1863–1877*. New York: Harper & Row Publishers. .

Foner, Eric (1990). *A Short History of Reconstruction 1863–1877*. New York: Harper & Row Publishers .

Foner, P. (1979) *Jamaica Farewell*. Jamaican Migrants in London: London: Routledge Kegan & Paul.

Foucault, Michel (1977). *Discipline and Punish: The Birth of the Prison* (Alan Sheridan, Trans.). London: Penguin Books.

Franklin, John Hope and Alfred A. Moss Jr. (2000). *From Slavery to Freedom: A History of African Americans* (Eighth Edition). New York: Alfred A. Knopf.

Fraser, Nancy (1997). *Justice Interruptus: Critical Reflections on the "Postsocialist" Condition*. New York & London: Routledge.

Frazier, Franklin E. (1939). *The Negro Family in America*. Chicago: University of Chicago Press.

Frazier, Franklin E. (1957). *Black Bourgeoisie: The Rise of a New Middle Class*. New York: The Free Press.

Frazier, Franklin E. (1968). *The Free Negro Family*. New York: Arno Press and The New York Times.

Freud, Sigmund (1989 [1940]. *An Outline of Psycho-Analysis* (James Strachey, Trans. and Editor). New York: W.W. Norton & Company.

Freud, Sigmund (1989 [1921]. *Group Psychology and the Analysis of the Ego* (James Strachey, Trans. and Editor). New York: W.W. Norton & Company.

Freud, Sigmund (1989 [1917]. *Introductory Lectures on Psycho-Analysis* (James Strachey, Trans. and Editor). New York: W.W. Norton & Company.

Fryer, P. (1984) *Staying Power: The History of Black People in Britain*. London: Pluto Press.

Gadamer, Hans-Georg (2002). *Truth and Method* (Second, Revised Edition, Joel Weinsheimer and Donald G. Marshall, Trans.). New York: Continuum.

Gartman, David (2002). "Bourdieu's Theory of Cultural Change: Explication, Application, Critique." *Sociological Theory* 20 (2): 255–277.

Gates, Henry L. et al. (Eds.) (1997). *The Norton Anthology: African American Literature* . New York: W.W. Norton & Company Inc.

Gates, Henry Louis, Jr. and Cornel West (1996). *The Future of the Race*. New York: Vintage Books.

Gilroy, P. (1990) 'The end of Anti-Racism.' *New Community*. 17 (1): pp. 71–83.

Geertz, Clifford (1973). *The Interpretation of Cultures*. New York: Basic Books.

Geertz, Clifford (2000). *Local Knowledge: Further Essays in Interpretive Anthropology*. New York: Basic Books.

Genovese, Eugene (1974). *Roll, Jordan, Roll*. New York: Pantheon Books.

Geronimus, Arline T. and F. Phillip Thompson. "To Denigrate, Ignore, or Disrupt: Racial Inequality in Health and the Impact of a Policy-induced Breakdown of African American Communities." *Du Bois Review* 1; 2: 247–279.

Giddens, Anthony (1984). *The Constitution of Society: Outline of the Theory of Structuration*. Cambridge: Polity Press.

Gilroy, Paul (1987) *There Ain't No Blacks in the Union Jack: The Cultural Politics of Race and Nation.* London: Routledge.

Gilroy, Paul (1993). *The Black Atlantic: Modernity and Double Consciousness*. Cambridge, Massachusetts: Harvard.

Glazer, Nathan and Daniel P. Moynihan (1963). *Beyond the Melting Pot*. Cambridge: Harvard University Press.

Gooding-Williams, Robert (1996). "Outlaw, Appiah, and Du Bois's 'The Conservation of Races.'" In Bell W. Bernard et al. (Eds.), *W.E.B. Du Bois on Race and Culture: Philosophy, Politics, and Poetics* (pp. 39–56). New York and London: Routledge.

Gramsci, Antonio (1959). *The Modern Prince, and Other Writings*. New York: International Publishers.

Greene, M. & Way, N. (2005) Self-Esteem Trajectories among Ethnic Minority Adolescents: A Growth Curve Analysis of the Patterns and Predictors of Change. *Journal of Research on Adolescence*, (15), 151–178.

Grutter v. Bollinger et al, 539 U.S. 02–241 (2003); 13 (Slip Opinion).

Gutiérrez, Ramón A. (2004). "Internal Colonialism: An American Theory of Race." *Du Bois Review*, 1; 2: 281–295.

Gutman, Herbert (1976). *The Black Family in Slavery and Freedom 1750–1925*. New York: Pantheon Books.

Habermas, Jürgen (1987). *The Theory of Communicative Action: Lifeworld and System: A Critique of Functionalist Reason* (Volume 2, Thomas McCarthy, Trans.). Boston: Beacon Press.

Habermas, Jürgen (1984). *The Theory of Communicative Action: Reason and the Rationalization of Society* (Volume 1, Thomas McCarthy, Trans.). Boston: Beacon Press.

Handlin, Oscar and Mary F. Handlin (1972). "The Origins of Negro Slavery." In Donald Noel (Ed.), *The Origins of American Slavery and Racism* (pp. 21–44). Ohio: Charles E. Merrill Publishing Co.

Harding, Vincent (1981). *There is a River: The Black Struggle for Freedom in America.* New York: Harcourt Brace & Company.

Hare, Nathan (1991). *The Black Anglo-Saxons.* Chicago: Third World Press.

Harris, Marvin. (1999). *Theories of culture in postmodern times.* Walnut Creek, California: AltaMira Press.

Harris, David R. and Jeremiah Joseph Sim (2002). "Who is Multiracial? Assessing the Complexity of Lived Race." *American Sociological Review* 67; 4: 614–627.

Heath, A. and Cheung, S. (2006) *Ethnic Penalties in the Labor Market: Employers and Discrimination.* Research report No 341. London: Department of Work and Pensions.

Heath, A. and Yu, S. (2005) *Explaining Ethnic Minority Disadvantage* (pp.187–224). In: Heath, A., Ermisch, J. and Gallie, D. *Understanding social change.* Oxford, Oxford University Press.

Hegel, G.W.F. (1977 [1807]). *Phenomenology of Spirit* (A.V. Miller, Trans.). Oxford: Oxford University Press.

Heidegger, Martin (1962 [1927]). *Being and Time.* New York: Harper San Francisco. Helle, H.J. and S.N. Eisenstadt (ed.) (1985). *Macro-Sociological Theory: Perspectives on Sociological Theory* (Volume 1). United Kingdom: J.W. Arrowsmith Ltd.

Helle, H.J. and S.N. Eisenstadt (ed.) (1985). *Micro-Sociological Theory: Perspectives on Sociological Theory* (Volume 2). United Kingdom: J.W. Arrowsmith Ltd.

Herskovits, Melville J. (1958 [1941]). *The Myth of the Negro Past.* Boston: Beacon Press.

Hewitt, R. (1986) *White Talk Black Talk: Inter-Racial Friendship and Communication amongst Adolescents.* Cambridge: Cambridge University Press.

Hiro, D. (1973*) Black British, White British.* Harmondsworth: Penguin.

HMSO (1991) *Aspects of Britain's Ethnic Minorities.* London: H.M.S.O.

Hochschild, Jennifer L. (1984). *The New American Dilemma: Liberal Democracy and School Desegregation.* New Haven: Yale University Press.

Hogue, Lawrence W. (1996). *Race, Modernity, Postmodernity: A look at the History and the Literatures of People of Color Since the 1960s.* Albany: State University of New York Press.

Holloway, Joseph E. (ed.) (1990a). *Africanisms in American Culture.* Bloomington and Indianapolis: Indiana University Press.

Holloway, Joseph E. (1990b). "The Origins of African-American Culture." In Joseph Holloway (Ed.), *Africanisms in American Culture* (19–33). Bloomington and Indianapolis: Indiana University Press.

Holt, Thomas (1990). "The Political Uses of Alienation: W.E.B. Du Bois on Politics, Race, and Culture, 1903–1940." *American Quarterly* 42 (2): 301–323.

Horkheimer, Max and Theodor W. Adorno (2000 [1944]. *Dialectic of Enlightenment* (John Cumming, Trans.). New York: Continuum.

Horne, Gerald (1986). *Black and Red: W.E.B. Du Bois and the Afro-American Response to the Cold War, 1944–1963.* New York: State University of New York Press.

House, James S. (1977). "The Three Faces of Social Psychology." *Sociometry* 40: 161–177.

House, James S. (1981). "Social Structure and Personality." In Morris Rosenberg and Ralph Turner (Eds.), *Sociological Perspectives on Social Psychology* (pp. 525–561). New York: Basic Books.

Hudson, Kenneth and Andrea Coukos (2005). "The Dark Side of the Protestant Ethic: A Comparative Analysis of Welfare Reform." *Sociological Theory* 23 (1): 1–24.

Hunton, Alphaeus w. (1970). "W.E.B. Du Bois: the meaning of his life." In John Henrik Clarke et al (Eds.), *Black Titan: W.E.B. Du Bois* (pp. 131–137). Boston: Beacon Press.

Inkeles, Alex (1959). "Personality and Social Structure." In Robert K. Merton, Leonard Broom, and Leonard S. Cottrell, Jr. (eds.), *Sociology Today* (pp. 249–276). New York: Basic Books.

Inkeles, Alex (1960). "Industrial man: The Relation of Status, Experience, and Value." *American Journal of Sociology* 66: 1–31.

Inkeles, Alex (1969). "Making Men Modern: On the causes and consequences of individual change in six developing countries." *American Journal of Sociology* 75: 208–225.

James, C.L.R., Breitman, G. & Keemer, E. (1980) Fighting Racism in World War 1. New York: Monad Press.

James, CLR (1986). *The Black Jacobins: Toussaint L' Ouverture and the San Domingo Revolution*. Vintage.

Jameson, Fredric and Masao Miyoshi (ed.). (1998). *The Cultures of Globalization*. Durham: Duke University Press.

Jones, G.S. (1971). *Outcast London: A Study in the Relationship Between Classes in Victorian Society*. Oxford: Clarendon Press.

Jordan, Winthrop D. (1972). "Modern Tensions and the Origins of American Slavery." In Donald Noel (Ed.), *The Origins of American Slavery and Racism* (pp. 81–94). Ohio: Charles E. Merrill Publishing Co.

Kardiner, Abram and Lionel Ovesey (1962 [1951]. *The Mark of Oppression: Explorations in the Personality of the American Negro*. Meridian Ed.

Karenga, Maulana (1993). *Introduction to Black Studies*. California: The University of Sankore Press.

Kellner, Douglas (2002). "Theorizing Globalization." *Sociological Theory*, 20: (3), 285–305.

Kneller, George F. (1964). *Introduction to the Philosophy of Education*. New York: John Wiley & Sons, Inc.

Kuhn, Thomas S. (1996). *The Structure of Scientific Revolutions* (Third Edition). Chicago: The University of Chicago Press.

Laclau, Ernesto and Chantal Mouffe (1985). *Hegemony & Socialist Strategy: Towards a Radical Democratic Politics*. New York and London: Verso.

Layton-Henry, Z. (1984) *The Politics of Race in Britain*. London: Allen & Unwin.

Lester, Julius (ed.) (1971). *The Seventh Son: The Thought and Writings of W.E.B. Du Bois* (Volume I). New York: Random House.

Lester, Julius (ed.) (1971). *The Seventh Son: The Thought and Writings of W.E.B. Du Bois* (Volume II). New York: Random House.

Lewis, David Levering (1993). *W.E.B. Du Bois: Biography of a Race 1868–1919*. New York: Henry Holt and Company.

Levine, Lawrence W. (1977). *Black Culture and Black Consciousness: Afro-American Folk Thought from Slavery to Freedom*. New York: Oxford University Press.

Lévi-Strauss, Claude (1963). *Structural Anthropology* (Claire Jacobson and Brooke Schoepf, Trans.). New York: Basic Books.

Lincoln, Eric C. and Lawrence H. Mamiya (1990). *The Black Church in the African American Experience*. Durham and London: Duke University Press.

Lowenthal, D. (1972) *West Indian Societies*. Oxford: Oxford University Press.

Luckmann, Thomas (Ed.) (1978). *Phenomenology and Sociology: Selected Readings*. New York: Penguin Books.

Lukács, Georg (1971). *History and Class Consciousness: Studies in Marxist Dialectics* (Rodney Livingstone, Trans.). Cambridge, Massachusetts: The MIT Press.

Lukács, Georg (2000). *A Defence of History and Class Consciousness: Tailism and the Dialectic* (Esther Leslie, Trans.). London and New York: Verso.

Luscombe, David (1997). *A History of Western Philosophy: Medieval Thought*. Oxford: Oxford University Press.

Lyman, Stanford M. (1997). *Postmodernism and a Sociology of the Absurd and Other Essays on the "Nouvelle Vague" in American Social Science*. Fayetteville: The University of Arkansas Press.

Lyman, Stanford M. and Arthur J. Vidich (1985). *American Sociology: Worldly Rejections of Religion and Their Directions*. New Haven and London: Yale University Press.

Lyman, Stanford M. (1972). *The Black American in Sociological Thought*. New York.

Mageo, Jeannette Marie (1998). *Theorizing Self in Samoa: Emotions, Genders, and Sexualities*. Ann Arbor: The University of Michigan Press.

Massey, D.S., and Denton, N.A. (1993). *American Apartheid: Segregation and the Making of the Underclass*. Cambridge, MA: Harvard University Press.

Marable, Manning (1986). *W.E.B. Du Bois: Black Radical Democrat*. Boston: Twayne Publishers.

Marcuse, Herbert (1964). *One-Dimensional Man*. Boston: Beacon Press.

Marcuse, Herbert (1974). *Eros and Civilization: A Philosophical Inquiry into Freud*. Boston: Beacon Press.

Marshall, Gordon (Ed.) (1998). *A Dictionary of Sociology* (Second edition). Oxford: Oxford University Press.

Martin, R. and Rowthorn, R, (Eds.) (1986) The Geography of Deindustrialization, London: Macmillan.

Marx, Karl and Friedrich Engels (1964). *The Communist Manifesto*. London, England: Penguin Books.

Marx, Karl (1992 [1867]). *Capital: A Critique of Political Economy* (Volume 1, Samuel Moore and Edward Aveling, Trans.). New York: International Publishers.

Marx, Karl (1998 [1845]). *The German Ideology*. New York: Prometheus Books.

Mason, Patrick L. (1996). "Race, Culture, and the Market." *Journal of Black Studies*, 26: 6, 782–808.

McMichael, Philip (2008). Development and Social Change: A Global Perspective. Los Angeles, California: Sage Publications.

Mead, George Herbert (1978 [1910]). "What Social Objects Must Psychology Presuppose." In Thomas Luckmann (Ed.), *Phenomenology and Sociology: Selected Readings* (17–24). New York: Penguin Books.

Meier, August (1963). *Negro Thought in America, 1880–1915: Racial Ideologies in the Age of Booker T. Washington*. Ann Arbor: The University of Michigan Press.

Meier, August and Elliott M. Rudwick (1976 [1966]). *From Plantation to Ghetto; an Interpretive History of American Negroes*. New York: Hill and Wang.

Métraux, Alfred (1958 [1989]). *Voodoo in Haiti*. New York: Pantheon Books.

Michel, Claudine (2006). Of Worlds Seen and Unseen: The Educational Character of Haitian Vodou." In Bellegarde-Smith, Patrick and Claudine Michel (eds.) *Haitian Vodou: Spirit, Myth, & Reality* (pgs. 32–44). Bloomington, IN: Indiana University Press.

Milner, D. (1975) *Children and Race*. Harmondsworth: Penguin.

Mirza, H. (2005) The more things change, the more they stay the same: Assessing Black Underachievement 35 years on. In B Richardson. (Ed.) *Tell it like it is. How our School fail Black Children* (pp.111–119). Stoke-on-Trent: Trentham Books.

Mocombe, Paul C., Carol Tomlin, Cecile Wright (2014). *Race and Class Distinctions Within Black Communities: A Racial Caste in Class*. Routledge Research in Race and Ethnicity (Vol. 9). New York and London: Routledge.

Mocombe, Paul C., Carol Tomlin, and Cecile Wright (2014). "A Racial Caste in Class: Race and Class Distinctions within Black Communities in the United States and United Kingdom." *Race, Gender, & Class*, 21, 3–4: 101–121.

Mocombe, Paul C., Carol Tomlin, and Cecile Wright (2014). "Race and Class Distinctions within Black Communities in the United States and United Kingdom: A Reading in Phenomenological Structuralism." *African and Black Diaspora: An International Journal.*

Mocombe, Paul C., Carol Tomlin, and Victoria Showunmi (2014). "Jesus and the Streets: A Hermeneutical Framework for Understanding the Intraracial Gender Academic Achievement Gap in Black Urban America and the United Kingdom." *Language and Sociocultural Theory*, 1, 2: 125–152.

Mocombe, Paul C., Carol Tomlin, and Cecile Wright (2014). "A Structural Approach to Understanding Black British Caribbean Academic Underachievement in the United Kingdom." *Journal of Social Science for Policy Implications*, 2, 2: 37–58.

Mocombe, Paul C., Carol Tomlin, and Cecile Wright (2013). "Karl Marx, Ludwig Wittgenstein, and Black Underachievement in the United States and United Kingdom." *Diaspora, Indigenous, and Minority Education*, 7, 4: 214–228.

Mocombe, Paul C., Carol Tomlin, and Cecile Wright (2013). "Postindustrial Capitalism, Social Class Language Games, and Black Underachievement in the United States and United Kingdom." *Mind, Culture, and Activity*, 20, 4: 358–371.

Mocombe, Paul C. and Carol Tomlin (2013). *Language, Literacy, and Pedagogy in Postindustrial Societies: The Case of Black Academic Underachievement*. Routledge Research in Education (Vol. 97). New York and London: Routledge.

Mocombe, Paul C. (2012). *Liberal Bourgeois Protestantism: The Metaphysics of Globalization*. Studies in Critical Social Sciences (Vol. 41). Leiden, Netherlands: Brill Publications.

Mocombe, Paul C. and Carol Tomlin (2010). *Oppositional Culture Theory*. Maryland: University Press of America.

Mocombe, Paul C. (2009). *The Liberal Black Protestant Heterosexual Bourgeois Male: From W.E.B. Du Bois to Barack Obama*. Maryland: University Press of America. Mocombe, Paul C. (2008). *The Soulless Souls of Black Folk: A Sociological Reconsideration of Black Consciousness as Du Boisian Double Consciousness*. Maryland: University Press of America.

Model, S. and Fisher, G. (2002) Unions between Blacks and Whites: England and the US Compared. *Ethnic and Racial Studies* 25 (5) pp 728–754.

Modood, T., Berthoud, R., Lakey, J., Nazroo, J., Smith, P., Virdee, S. and Beishon, S. (1997) *Ethnic Minorities in Britain: Diversity and Disadvantage*. Policy Studies Institute, London.

Moore, Jerry D. (1997). *Visions of Culture: An Introduction to Anthropological Theories and Theorists*. Walnut Creek, California: AltaMira Press.

Moynihan, Daniel P. (1965). The Negro Family. Washington, D.C.: Office of Planning and Research, US Department of Labor.

Mullard, C. (1982) 'Multiracial Education in Britain: from Assimilation to Cultural Pluralism' in J. (Ed.) (1982) Race, Migration and Schooling.pp.120–33. London: Holt, Rinehart and Winston.

Murray, Charles (1984). *Losing Ground: American Social Policy 1950–1980*. New York: Basic Books.

Murray, R.N. & Gbedemah, G.L (1983) *Foundations of Education in the Caribbean*. London: Hodder & Stoughton.

Myrdal, Gunnar (1944). *An American Dilemma: The Negro Problem and Modern Democracy*. New York: Harper & Row Publishers.

Nash, Gary B. (1972). "Red, White and Black: The Origins of Racism in Colonial America." In Donald Noel (Ed.), *The Origins of American Slavery and Racism* (pp. 131–152). Ohio: Charles E. Merrill Publishing Co.

Nicholls, David (1979). *From Dessalines to Duvalier: Race, Colour, and National Independence in Haiti*. New Jersey: Rutgers University Press.

Nietzsche, Friedrich (1956). *The Birth of Tragedy* and *The Genealogy of Morals* (Francis Golffing, Trans.). New York: Anchor Books.

Nobles, Wade (1987). *African American Families: Issues, Ideas, and Insights*. Oakland: Black Family Institute.

Noel, Donald L. (Ed.) (1972). *The Origins of American Slavery and Racism*. Columbus, Ohio: Charles E. Merrill Publishing Co.

Noel, Donald L. (1972). "A Theory of the Origins of Ethnic Stratification." In Donald Noel (Ed.), *The Origins of American Slavery and Racism* (pp. 106–127). Ohio: Charles E. Merrill Publishing Co.

Noel, Donald L. (1972). "Slavery and the Rise of Racism." In Donald Noel (Ed.), *The Origins of American Slavery and Racism* (pp. 153–174). Ohio: Charles E. Merrill Publishing Co.

Obeyesekere, Gananath (1997 [1992]). *The Apotheosis of Captain Cook: European Mythmaking in the Pacific*. Hawaii: Bishop Museum Press.

Ortner, Sherry (1984). "Theory in Anthropology Since the Sixties," *Comparative Studies in Society and History* 26: 126–66.

Outlaw, Lucius (1996). "Conserve" Races?: In Defense of W.E.B. Du Bois." In Bernard W. Bell et al (Eds.), *W.E.B. Du Bois on Race and Culture: Philosophy, Politics, and Poetics* (pp. 15–38). New York and London: Routledge.

Parsons, Talcott (1951). *The Social System*. Glencoe, Illinois: Free Press.

Parsons, Talcott (1954). *Essays in Sociological Theory*. Glencoe, Illinois: Free Press.

Parsons, Talcott (1977). *Social Systems and the Evolutions of Action Theory*. New York: Free Press.

Patterson, Orlando (1982). *Slavery and Social Death: A Comparative Study*. Cambridge, Massachusetts: Harvard University Press.

Peach, C. (1968) *West Indian Migration to Britain*: A Social Geography. London: Oxford University Press.

Peach, C. (Ed.) (1996a) *The Ethnic Minority Populations of Great Britain*: Volume 2 of the Ethnicity in the 1991 Census. Office for National Statistics. London: HMSO.

Phillips, U.B. (1918). *American Negro Slavery: A survey of the Supply, Employment, and Control of Negro Labor as Determined by the Plantation Regime*. New York: D. Appleton and Company.

Phillips, U.B. (1963). *Life and Labor in the Old South*. Boston: Little Brown.

Pierre-Louis, Francois (2000). "Decentralization and Democracy in Haiti," paper presented at the International Conference on Democratic Decentralization May 23rd-29th, 2000 Kerala, India.

Polanyi, Karl (2001 [1944]). *The Great Transformation: The Political and Economic Origins of Our Time*. Boston: Beacon Press.

Pollard, V. (1994). *Dread Talk: The Language of Rastafari*. Barbados, Jamaica, Trindad and Tobago: Canoe Press.

Power, S., Edwards, T., Whitty, G. & Wigfall, V. (2003) *Education and the Middle Class* Buckingham, Milton Keynes: Open University Press.

Price-Mars, Jean (1928). Ainsi Parla L' Oncle. Port-au-Prince: Imprimeria de Compiégne.

Psathas, George (1989). *Phenomenology and Sociology: Theory and Research*. Washington, D.C.: University Press of America.

Ramsey, Kate (2014). *The Spirits and the Law: Vodou and Power in Haiti*. Chicago: University of Chicago Press.

Rao, Hayagreeva et al (2005). "Border Crossing: Bricolage and the Erosion of Categorical Boundaries in French Gastronomy," *American Sociological Review* 70: 968–991.

Reed, Adolph L. (1997). *W.E.B. Du Bois and American Political Thought: Fabianism and the Color Line*. New York and Oxford: Oxford University Press.

Reyna, Stephen P. (1997). "Theory in Anthropology in the Nineties," *Cultural Dynamics* 9 (3): 325–350.

Rex, J. & Moore, R. (1967) *Race, Community & Conflict*. London: Oxford University Press.

Rigaud, Milo (1985). *Secrets of Voodoo*. San Francisco, CA: City Lights Books.

Roediger, David R. (1999). *The Wages of Whiteness: Race and the Making of the American Working Class*. London and New York: Verso.

Rose, Sonya O. (1997). "Class Formation and the Quintessential Worker." In John R. Hall (Ed.), *Reworking Class* (pp. 133–166). Ithaca and London: Cornell University Press.

Rosen, H., and Burgess T. (1980). *Language and Dialects of London School Children*. London: Ward, Lock Educational.

Rosenau, Pauline Marie (1992). *Post-Modernism and the Social Sciences: Insights, Inroads, and Intrusions*. Princeton, New Jersey: Princeton University Press.

Roumain, Jacques S. (1940). "The Southeast and the West Indies." *In Prehistoric Patterns in the New World*, edited by Gordon R. Wiley, 165–72. New York: Viking Fund Publications in Anthropology.

Rubin, Vera (Ed.) (1960). *Caribbean Studies: A Symposium*. Seattle: University of Washington Press.

Sahlins, Marshall (1995a). *How "Natives" Think: About Captain Cook, For Example*. Chicago: University of Chicago Press.

Sahlins, Marshall (1995b). *Historical Metaphors and Mythical Realities*. Ann Arbor: University of Michigan Press.

Sahlins, Marshall (1990). "The Political Economy of Grandeur in Hawaii from 1810 1830." In Emiko Ohnuki-Tierney (Ed.), *Culture through Time: Anthropological Approaches* (pp. 26–56). California: Stanford University Press.

Sahlins, Marshall (1989). "Captain Cook at Hawaii," *The Journal of the Polynesian Society* 98; 4: 371–423.

Sahlins, Marshall (1985). *Islands of History*. Chicago: University of Chicago Press.

Sahlins, Marshall (1982). "The Apotheosis of Captain Cook." In Michel Izard and Pierre Smith (Eds.), *Between Belief and Transgression* (pp. 73–102). Chicago: University of Chicago Press.

Sahlins, Marshall (1976). *Culture and Practical Reason*. Chicago, IL: University of Chicago Press.

Said, Edward (1979). *Orientalism*. New York: Vintage Books.

Sarup, Madan (1993). *An Introductory Guide to Post-Structuralism and Postmodernism* (second edition). Athens: The University of Georgia Press.

Saussure de, Ferdinand (1972 [1916]. *Course in General Linguistics*, Edited by Charles Bally et al. Illinois: Open Court.

Sertima, Ivan V. ([1979] 1989). *They Came Before Columbus*. New York: Random House.

Schutz, Alfred (1978). "Phenomenology and the Social Sciences." In Thomas Luckmann (Ed.), *Phenomenology and Sociology: Selected Readings* (pp. 119–141). New York: Penguin Books.

Schutz, Alfred (1978). "Some Structures of the Life-World." In Thomas Luckmann (Ed.), *Phenomenology and Sociology: Selected Readings* (pp. 257–274). New York: Penguin Books.

Schwalbe, Michael L. (1993). "Goffman Against Postmodernism: Emotion and the Reality of the Self." *Symbolic Interaction* 16(4): 333–350.

Searle, John R. (1997). *The Mystery of Consciousness*. New York: The New York Review of Books.

Sebba, M. (1993). *London Jamaican*. London: Longman.

Sebba, M. (2007) *Caribbean Creoles and Black English*. In D. Britain (Ed.) *Languages in the British Isles: Language in the British Isles*. (pp. 276–292). Cambridge: Cambridge University Press.

Sennett, Richard (1998). *The Corrosion of Character*. New York: W.W. Norton & Company.

Slemon, Stephen (1995). "The Scramble for Post-colonialism." In Bill Ashcroft et al (Eds.), The Post-colonial Studies Reader (pp. 45–52). London and New York: Routledge.

Smedley, Audrey (1999). *Race in North America: Origin and Evolution of a Worldview* (Second edition). Boulder, Colorado: Westview Press.

Smiley Group, Inc. (2006). *The Covenant with Black America*. Chicago: Third World Press.

Smith M.G. (1960). "The African Heritage in the Caribbean." In Vera Rubin (Ed.), *Caribbean Studies: A Symposium* (pp. 34–46). Seattle: University of Washington Press.

Solomon, Robert C. (1988). *A History of Western Philosophy: Continental Philosophy Since 1750, The Rise and Fall of the Self*. Oxford: Oxford University Press.

Sowell, Thomas (1975). *Race and Economics*. New York: David McKay.

Sowell, Thomas (1981). *Ethnic America*. New York: Basic Books.

Spivak, Chakravorty Gayatri (1994 [1988]). "Can the Subaltern Speak?" In Patrick Williams and Laura Chrisma (Eds.), *Colonial Discourse and Post-Colonial Theory A Reader* (pp. 66–111). New York: Columbia University Press.

Stack, Carol B. (1974). *All Our Kin: Strategies for Survival in a Black Community*. New York: Harper & Row Publishers.

Stampp, Kenneth (1967). *The Peculiar Institution*. New York: Alfred Knopf, Inc.

Strand, S. (2012) The White British-Black Caribbean Achievement Gap: Tests, Tiers and Teacher Expectations. *British Educational Research Journal* 28 (1): pp. 75–101.

Staples, Robert (ed.) (1978). *The Black Family: Essays and Studies*. California Wadsworth Publishing Company.

Stewart, David and Algis Mickunas (1990). *Exploring Phenomenology: A Guide to the Field and its Literature* (Second edition). Athens: Ohio University Press.

Strauss, Claudia and Naomi Quinn (1997). *A Cognitive Theory of Cultural Meaning*. United Kingdom: Cambridge University Press.

Stone, M. (1981) *Education and the Black Child: the Myth of Multicultural Education*. London: Fontana.

Stuckey, Sterling (1987). *Slave Culture: Nationalist Theory and the Foundations of Black America*. New York and Oxford: Oxford University Press.

Sturrock, John (ed.) (1979). *Structuralism and Since: From Lévi-Strauss to Derrida*. Oxford: Oxford University Press.

Sudarkasa, Niara (1980). "African and Afro-American Family Structure: A Comparison," The *Black Scholar*, 11: 37–60.

Sudarkasa, Niara (1981). "Interpreting the African Heritage in Afro-American Family Organization." In Harriette P. McAdoo (Ed.), *Black Families*. California: Sage Publications.

Sundquist, Eric J. (ed.) (1996). *The Oxford W.E.B. Du Bois Reader*. New York and Oxford: Oxford University Press.

Sutcliffe, D. (1992). *Systems in Black Language*. Avon, Clevedon: Multilingual Matters.

Swann Report (1985) *Education for all: Report of the Committee of Inquiry into the Education of children from Minority Ethnic Groups*. London: HMSO.

Thomas, Nicholas (1982). "A Cultural Appropriation of History? Sahlins Among the Hawaiians," *Canberra Anthropology* 5; 1: 60–65.

Thompson, E.P. (1964). *The Making of the English Working Class*. New York: Pantheon Books.

Thompson, E.P. (1978). *The Poverty of Theory and Other Essays*. New York: Monthly Review Press.

Tomlin, C. (1988). "Black Preaching Style". MPhil thesis. University of Birmingham, Birmingham.

Tomlin, C. (1999). *Black Language Style in Sacred and Secular Contexts*. Medgar Evers College (CUNY): Caribbean Diaspora Press.

Tomlinson, S. (1984) *Home and School in Multicultural Britain*. London: Batsford.

Tomlinson, S. (2001) Education in a Post-welfare Society. Buckingham: Open University Press.

Tomlinson, S. (2008) *Race & Education: Policy & Politics in Britain*. Maidenhead, Berkshire: Open University Press.

Tomlinson, S. (2011) More Radical Reform (but don't mention race) Gaps and Silences in the Government's Discourse. *Race Equality Teaching* 29 (2): 25–29.

Townsend, H.E.R. (1971) Immigrants in England: The LEA Response: Slough: National Foundation for Educational Research.

Trouillot, Michel-Rolph (1995). *Silencing the Past: Power and the Production of History*. Boston, Massachusetts: Beacon Press.

Troyna, B. (1979) Differential Commitment to Ethnic Identity by Black Youths in Britain. *New Community* (7): 406–414.

Troyna, B. (1993) *Racism and Education: Research Perspectives*. Buckingham: Open University Press.

Troyna, B. Smith, D.I. (Eds.) (1983) *Racism, School and the Labor Market*. Leicester: National Youth Bureau.

Troyna, B. and Carrington, B. (1990) *Education, Racism and Reform*: London: Routledge.

Trudgill, P. (1990). *Sociolinguistics: An Introduction*. Harmondsworth: Penguin.

Tulloch, Hugh (1999). *The Debate on the American Civil War Era*. Manchester: Manchester University Press.

Turner, Ralph H. (1976). "The Real Self: From Institution to Impulse." *American Journal of Sociology* 81: 989–1016.

Turner, Ralph H. (1988). "Personality in Society: Social Psychology's Contribution to Sociology." *Social Psychology Quarterly* 51; 1: 1–10.

Tussman, Joseph and Jacobus TenBroek (1949). "The Equal Protection of the Laws." *California Law Review* 37;3:341–381.

Wallerstein, Immanuel (1982). "The Rise and Future Demise of the World Capitalist System: Concepts for Comparative Analysis." In Hamza Alavi and Teodor Shanin (Eds.), *Introduction to the Sociology of "Developing Societies"* (pp. 29–53). New York: Monthly Review Press.

Walvin, J. (1984) Passage to Britain. Harmondsworth: Penguin.

Walvin, J. (1982) Black Ivory: A History of British Slavery. London: Harper Collins.

Ward, Glenn (1997). *Postmodernism*. London: Hodder & Stoughton Ltd.

Warren, S. and Gillborn, D. (2003). *Race Equality and Education in Birmingham*. London: Education Policy Research Unit, Institute of Education.

Watkins, S. Craig (1998). *Representing: Hip-Hop Culture and the Production of Black Cinema*. Chicago: The University of Chicago Press.

Weber, Max (1958 [1904–1905]). *The Protestant Ethic and the Spirit of Capitalism* (Talcott Parsons, Trans.). New York: Charles Scribner's Sons.

Weinreich, U. (1968). *Language in Contact*. The Hague: Mouton.

West, Cornel (1993). *Race Matters*. New York: Vintage Books.

West, David (1996). *An Introduction to Continental Philosophy*. Cambridge: Polity Press.

Williams, Raymond (1977). *Marxism and Literature*. Oxford: Oxford University Press.

Wilson, Kirt H. (1999). "Towards a Discursive Theory of Racial Identity: The Souls of Black Folk as a Response to Nineteenth-Century Biological Determinism." *Western Journal of Communication*, 63 (2): 193–215.

Wilson, William J. (1978). *The Declining Significance of Race: Blacks and Changing American Institutions*. Chicago and London: The University of Chicago Press.

Wilson, William J. (1987). *The Truly Disadvantaged*. Chicago and London: University of Chicago Press.

Winant, Howard (2001). *The World is a Ghetto: Race and Democracy since World War II*. New York: Basic Books.

Winford, D. (1993). *Predication in Caribbean Creoles*. Amsterdam: John Benjamins.

Wittgenstein, Ludwig (2001 [1953]). *Philosophical Investigations* (G.E.M. Anscombe Trans.). Malden, Massachusetts: Blackwell Publishers Ltd.

Wright, Kai (Ed.) (2001). *The African-American Archive: The History of the Black Experience in Documents*. New York: Black Dog & Leventhal Publishers.

Woodson, Carter G. (1969 [1933]). *The Mis-Education of the Negro*. Washington: Associated Publishers Inc.

Youdell, D. (2003) Identity Traps or How Black Students Fail: The Interaction Between Biographical, Sub-cultural and Learner Identities. *British Journal of Sociology of Education* 24 (1): 3–20.

Young, Iris Marion (1994). "Gender as Seriality: Thinking about Women as a Social Collective," *Signs* 19: 713–738.

Zamir, Shamoon (1995). *Dark Voices: W.E.B. Du Bois and American Thought, 1888–1903*. Chicago & London: The University of Chicago Press.

Zeitlin, Irving M. (1990). *Ideology and the development of sociological theory* (4th ed.). Englewood Cliffs, New Jersey: Prentice-Hall.

Index

www.ingramcontent.com/pod-product-compliance
Lightning Source LLC
Chambersburg PA
CBHW030653270326
41929CB00007B/350